LORE OF THE LAKE COUNTRY

LORE OF THE
LAKE COUNTRY

F.J. CARRUTHERS

LONDON
ROBERT HALE & COMPANY

ISBN 0 7091 4915 8

Robert Hale & Company
63 Old Brompton Road
London S.W.7

TO MADELINE

Computer typeset by Specialised Offset Services Ltd
and printed in Great Britain by
Redwood Burn Limited, Trowbridge & Esher

CONTENTS

ACKNOWLEDGEMENTS

The author wishes to thank Mr and Mrs John Richardson, of the Fish Hotel, Buttermere, for permission to reproduce the pictures of the Beauty of Buttermere; Manchester Corporation Waterworks Committee for permission to roam their country around Thirlmere; the Reverend Geoffrey White, of Loweswater, for information about the Loweswater chalice; the staff at the Cumberland County Archives at Carlisle Castle, and of the Library at Tullie House, and the Librarians and staff at the Workington and Whiteheaven libraries.

My thanks also to Sir John Burgess, chairman of Cumberland Newspapers Limited, for permission to use material which has, in other forms been published in the *Cumberland News*.

ILLUSTRATIONS

INTRODUCTION

The march of England's history has mostly by-passed the Lake Country. The Young Pretender, heading south to claim the Crown, followed the route of the modern A6, which, between Penrith and Kendal can be called the Lakes by-pass, reinforced now by the M6 motorway. Agricola, heading north to establish a north-west frontier of the Roman Empire, followed the coastal route, although a diversion was made to cross Hardknott Pass and provide a fort to guard it. The last Earl of Derwentwater, before he lost his all, head included, in the doomed cause of the Old Pretender, had severed his residential connection with Keswick and either came (or sent) for the rents of his extensive estates in the district.

Mary Queen of Scots merely touched the edge of the district when, at Workington and Cockermouth, she savoured her last experience of real English hospitality at the hands of the Cumbrians Curwen and Fletcher, after which she became a prisoner. The good and ever-acquisitive Queen Bess, in a notorious manoeuvre appropriated the Newlands mines because an obviously phoney assay of their product showed that the gold and silver won from the mine would yield greater returns than the base metals, copper and lead. By definition this made them 'Mines Royal' which was justification enough for them to be taken by the Crown, but the real reason, though not declared at the time for political reasons, was that the Queen and her advisers were in the process of needling her principal foe, the Earl of Northumberland, owner of the mines by birthright, into the action which became the Rebellion of the Northern Earls, and ended in the objective being achieved when Percy's head was displayed on a spike on one of the gates of York.

If history has mainly passed by the Lake District, fame has been achieved by some of its natives; international and durable if we take Wordsworth as an example; transient if we consider the case of Mary, the Beauty of Buttermere.

It also produced John Peel who hunted foxes, and John Woodcock Graves who ensured his immortality by writing the famous song about him. And it must be of some interest to lovers of the Lake Country that Cockermouth gave birth to John Grave, who performed a Dick Whittington act, became thrice Lord Mayor of Manchester, and traitorously (in the eyes of posterity) gave Thirlmere to Manchester, or at least sold them the idea of turning this pearl among lakes into a reservoir.

It gave birth to the legends of the Borrowdale 'gowks'; provided a setting for the tall stories of Auld Will Ritson, of Wasdale Head, and in its folklore was found the inspiration for even greater flights of fancy from the pens of visiting writers like Scott and Tennyson. Enthusiasm spread to amateur bards and visiting professionals, and local legends, like that about the sunken town in Mockerkin Tarn, were magnified to epic proportions, culminating in a whole volume of Scott-like effusions by William Pagan White, *Lays and Legends of the Lake Country*, which gained wide circulation a century or so ago.

That was not the end of it. If recent performance is anything by which to judge, the Lake Country is still building up a sort of spurious folklore. It was fortunate that the National Trust, who own the district, intervened in time to discourage visitors from believing that Judith Paris was a real person who actually lived at Watendlath. The encouragement had come from a notice board announcing that John Greenhouse Farm was "The home of Judith Paris", which was as good a way as any of drawing visitors in for afternoon tea when Walpole was a 'fashionable' novelist, and Clark Gable starred as Rogue Herries in *Vanessa*. The then owners of John Greenhouse Farm were, however, not altogether wrong, because it was there that Walpole soaked up atmosphere and dreamed up characters for his novels.

Obviously this book cannot deal with all the lore, folk and otherwise, of the Lake Country, which is fortunate in a way because some of the folklore is so obviously phoney that it is not worth bothering about. Much of it was produced almost 'to order' as a sort of early-day tourist trap by a people to whom the telling of tall stories was almost a way of life, a facet of their character which was revealed to a procession of discoverers of Lakeland beginning with people like George Smith who essayed that death defying trip into the Honister Fells in 1749 and Gray who ventured no farther than Grange in 1796.

I start with the Loweswater-Crummock-Buttermere (always strictly in that order for any Cumbrian) valley because it is my favourite place, where my love of the Lake Country was generated in countless days spent watching buzzard, raven and peregrine; climbing in Burtness Combe; picking bleaberries (bilberries, whinberries or whortleberries to the off-comer), and where for a day, at a very tender age when, unroped because I had not recognised the danger in the project, I went up Grassmoor Gully and was bitten by the rock-climbing bug.

John Peel could not be left out, not least because of that great day in 1954 which left a permanent mark on the memories of everybody there.

The generally-accepted 'life' of John Woodcock Graves, who wrote "D'ye ken John Peel" is contained in the auto-biographical notes he contributed to *Songs and Ballads of Cumberland* in which he villifies the wife to whom he and his family owed so much, and displays a condescension towards John Peel which angered Peel's family. Graves's life in Tasmania has no connection with Cumbria except in that he and his family kept constantly in touch with the home country, but is worth recording because, from the pen of his own daughter, Mary Amnie Hubbard, it reveals the waywardness of the man and puts into perspective the 'life' Graves wrote for Gilpin.

Mary Robinson, the Beauty of Buttermere, was an early case of the 'instant stardom' generally thought to be a twentieth-century phenomenon, and she is interesting, not so much for her involvement with the swindler Hatfield, as for the effect she had upon such celebrities as Wordsworth, Coleridge and de Quincey.

I tried to write about Borrowdale without bringing the 'wadd' into it, but the stuff tends to intrude upon the Borrowdale scene at any historical age. And if Borrowdale wadd demands attention there is, surely, interest in John Postlethwaite's theory 'that it was only by accident, during the great volcanic upheaval which formed the Lake Country mountains and tangled the district's geology, that the wadd did not turn into diamonds.

The Cumbrian natives' self-sufficiency included the production of homespun entertainment for special occasions, the best descriptions of these coming from the dialect poets with Wordsworth chipping in with, for him, a rollicking passage in "The Waggonner" about the dance at Wythburn's Cherry Tree Inn. Despite the volume of literature on the subject, the dance –and by that I mean the whole event and not individual performances – is difficult to reconstruct, but a clear picture has been left of the principal performer, the fiddler, by Alexander Craig Gibson whose monograph on Ben Wells and its accompanying dialect poem go some way towards filling an undoubted gap in the literature of the district.

Until I read Gibson I thought that Southey was the only other writer to take the trouble to discover more about the couple who, living in typically Wordsworthian Lakeland bliss above Langdale, deserved such a lot of time and space in *The Excursion*. It was natural that the author of "Joe and the Geologist" should see the grey comedy in the life of Betty and Jonathan Yewdale.

Jonathan Otley, the Keswick 'clocker' who fathered Lakeland geology, also confirmed that Derwentwater had an island which really floated. It is still there, but is has, publicity-wise, gone into eclipse because the late Charles Bone is no longer there to record its appearances and disappearances as faithfully as ever Jonathan Otley did, albeit less in the interest of science than in linage in the national newspapers.

Nobody has ever claimed that the fleece of a Herdwick sheep is golden, but the man who came nearest to turning that mass of steel-wool-coloured fibre into that ideal was Ned Nelson of Gatesgarth, surely one of the most important of all

Lakeland 'characters' for his efforts, against formidable opposition, to establish the Herdwick in its correct place as the premier breed of sheep for these mountainous parts.

For its name, and its proximity to the 'Celtic' parts of Lakeland, the Vale of St John and its Castle Rock have been credited with magical qualities by many writers, Scott included. But its real magic came from the mind and the pen of John Richardson whose dialect poetry has a delicacy and tenderness which nobody else had been able to draw from a folk speech which seems to have been designed for fratching and fighting since it contains no fewer than 109 words meaning 'beating' or 67 ways of calling a man (or woman) a fool.

In dozens of lectures I have given on Cumbria and its lore, mention of the local pearl fishery has raised a few eyebrows, but fishing for pearls in Cumberland rivers has at times been a lucrative business, depending upon how hard the times, how dedicated the fishermen.

I have given the title "Another World" to my chapter on Thirlmere because the more obvious "Lost World" has been used by other writers about this lake and about Haweswater, Manchester's other victim. Lost the old world around Thirlmere certainly is, and the loss is the greater for the 'other worldliness' of the district, evidence of which is found in ancient writings as well as in the customs of its inhabitants. In anything approaching its original condition, Celtic bridge and all, Thirlmere could today be a queen of the lakes instead of being so obviously a reservoir. Though, admittedly, it could also have been spoiled, by over exploitation — its farms and most of its houses in the hands of off-comers as holiday or retirement homes. Ninety years of expanding holiday usage would certainly have polished off the rough edges of life in the City of Wythburn and laid the ghosts of Armboth eternally to rest. And the Rock of Names would surely have been covered by the graffitti of less distinguished hands than those who carved the first initials on it.

Research material for this book has included everything about Cumbria and the Lake Country on which I could lay my hands, but the principal source has been the files of the old *West Cumberland Times*, of which I was editor for twenty-two years, and which has almost always, apparently, been edited with a view to somebody like myself coming to it in quest of information about bygone times and long-dead people.

1

Ninian's Valley?

High in the sky a buzzard wheels its lazy circles, its mewing call sounding mournful to the human listener, but probably bringing comfort to its mate sitting their two eggs on a vast nest in a tall pine in the lakeside forest. Up the valley, on sway-backed Melbreak's northern flank a peregrine falcon chitters its alarm note as a shepherd, invading its domain whistles control over three dogs raking sheep off the fellside. A pair of ravens, their almost-grown family satisfied for the time being, take time off for fun, indulging in the aerobatics they enjoyed during their courtship to the accompaniment of deep-throated chuckles which come clearly through the still air of the spring afternoon.

Where Nature is concerned, little has changed in the valley which holds the triplet lakes of Loweswater, Crummock and Buttermere. Buzzards and peregrines have been doing almost exactly the same things in almost exactly the same places since time began. So have ravens, but these great sable scavengers of the fellsides seem to demand less territorial rights, are less hostile to intruders and more a part of the scenery than their neighbours because, they have been there longer. They could be the valley's oldest inhabitants.

Redstarts flick their tails on wrecked dry-stone walls at the ruined farm of Bargate; elegant pied flycatchers dart from bough to lichen-dripping bough in the remnant of primaeval forest at the foot of Melbreak; a dipper strolls nonchalantly into the crystal-clear, ice-cold water of Mosedale beck to seek caddis grubs, and wheatears, home again after migration

15

make noises in the scree like stone tapping stone.

Foxes abound, badgers survive, and even the pine marten is making a come-back. This valley is one of few places where Nature, if not exactly winning the battle against progress and development, is at least holding her own.

Only people and the things people do have changed. In winter there are fewer people than there used to be; in summer there are more. There are fewer acres under the plough, more cows in the field; fewer Herdwick sheep competing for the forage of the fells, more cattle fattening on the valley bottom.

In a short lifetime the accents of the residents have changed, and the homely Cumberland dialect is disappearing. Houses for sale are bought by off-comers as holiday or retirement homes. Sons and daughters of native dalesmen cannot match the inflated prices property fetches at auction, and so, as the native stocks of Herdwicks roam the fells in diminishing numbers, the native stock of dalesmen is diminishing too. A cottage for sale becomes somebody's holiday home; a farm for sale turns into an investment for the future, stops being a farm, and brings in thirty pounds a week when let to holidaymakers. The land is let to other farmers whose farms thereupon become more viable. Raising beef on flat fields is a more commercial proposition than breeding Herdwicks on fellsides, and less hard work.

These changes in local farm economy make small impact on the valley scenery except that on the fellsides the dry-stone walls are crumbling because there are no longer men with the time or the inclination — or the skill — to mend them, and because, truth to tell, there is no longer any need for them. Boundaries between heafs are not now as finely drawn as they used to be when the statesmen had to count every square yard of grazing available to their flocks, and pay penalties if they put out too many sheep on the fell. There is no danger that the number of Herwicks grazing the heafs today will eat the fellsides bare.

There have been changes too among the clusters of farm buildings snug in their sycamore shelter belts where, in the scramble to find a place in this particularly lovely part of the country, barns have been made into better houses than those which have been home for many generations of dalesmen.

The pattern is repeated throughout the Lake Country, but in this valley the changes are perhaps not so great as elsewhere because there is little that can, or will be allowed to change. The Lake District Planning Board, the National Trust and the Friends of the Lake District are on guard protecting it more carefully because it is one of few places, even in the Lake District, which can still be called 'unspoiled'.

Unspoiled despite Crummock Water being used as a reservoir for West Cumberland towns and villages. Crummock has provided water for Workington almost as long as Thirlmere has performed a similar service for Manchester, but the differences between the two are great. A dalesman of a century ago would still recognise Crummock; an old-time dweller in Wythburn City would not recognise Thirlmere. Time and Nature have dealt gently with the Crummock waterworks and even the spillovers where the Cocker leaves the lake seem now to have blended into the landscape.

The old lore of this valley is of St Ninian, Ned Nelson and the Beauty of Buttermere; of the de Lindsays who once owned it and 'Wonderful' Walker who started his career there.[1]

Traditionally St Ninian came to this valley to preach and to convert the natives. The name remains at the well, or spring on Fangs Brow where he is said to have baptised his converts. As far back as folk memory goes this has been St Ninian's Well, or St Ringan's Well — a natural choice since the old Celtic saint has been given both these names.

Did he come here? Some antiquarians and archaeologists scoff at the idea. Ninian is so closely linked with the early Celtic Church in Scotland, and particularly in Galloway, that it seems inconceivable that he could have laboured anywhere but among his beloved Picts. There is an opinion today, however, that Ninian was Cumbrian-born, the son of a Romano-British chieftain who owed his power to his collaboration with the Roman army occupying the Wall and the coastal forts.

Aelred, a monk of Rievaux, reports that it was "in a region in the West part of the island, where at the present time an arm of the sea separates the realms of the Scots and the Angles, and which formerly had a king of its own, that the blessed Ninian sprang." The description fits Cumberland.

Ninian was born about AD 360 when Christianity was already an accepted religion of the Roman Empire. He seems to have been born a Christian, and having shown leanings towards teaching his religion he was sent to Rome to complete his training. He was then given his charge to return and teach his own people before moving on to his destiny with the southern Picts of Scotland.

The early 90s of the fourth century found Ninian back among his people rooting out what had been ill-planted, scattering what had been ill-gathered, and casting down what had been ill-built. It seems that the Christians in Ninian's native country had deviated somewhat from the true faith, and not for the last time – St Kentigern paid his historic visit to the region three centuries later with the same objects in view.

Only a few place names have handed down the Ninian tradition in Cumbria. No definite Ninian site has been identified; nothing has been discovered of anything which could be associated with the saint. The Ninian Well at Loweswater, Ninewells at Brisco near Brampton with the Ninian Oak nearby; the remote little church of Ninekirks on the Eamont near Brougham, and Martindale at Ullswater are places linked with the Ninian tradition, but that is all. If Ninian was a Cumbrian, 'his' people would live on the Romantised coastal strip, but if he was the man his biographers have made of him he had zeal and energy enough to take him into the Cumbrian hinterland whose people were closely related to his tribe.

If Ninian's Well on Fangs Brow does not fit the popular image of a holy well, even less so does the Lord's Well in Mosedale which runs between Melbreak and Hen Comb. Bricked round and with a piece of corrugated iron for cover it is a water supply for Kirkhead. In its original state it was a spring of clear water gushing out from the foot of Melbreak, in which condition it would fit exactly the requirements of early evangelists in the mould of Ninian or Kentigern. But who named the Lord's Well, and why, remains a mystery. It could have been an early Christian teacher and baptiser, or it could have been named by some latter-day Loweswater priest who drew water there for church purposes.

The influence of the Church is obvious in the place-names in the small areas between the hamlet of Kirkstile and the mouth of Mosedale. Kirkstile itself: the name of the hamlet and the inn; Kirkhead, the farm up Chapel Lonning from Kirkstile, and on Kirkhead farm is Kirkstead 'the place of the Church', the valley's greatest puzzle.

Kirkstead is a great raised work of small stones, now grassed over. Roughly rectangular, it is about 150 by 80 feet. The rampart is on three sides of the rectangle only, and outside the south-western corner is a smaller enclosure measuring 40 by 15 feet. Tradition says that this is the remains of a church, and the name, and the east-west orientation suggests that this might be so, or at least that the structure has had some association with Christian worship. The fact that the east end of the Kirkstead is open lends a little weight to the tradition, but the fact that there is no east wall — and there are no signs of there ever having been one — could also point towards something to do with sun worship. That the smaller rectangle appended to the bigger work has been called the 'Vestry' is meaningless when it is known that the small enclosure within the stone circle at Castlerigg, Keswick, has also been called a vestry. Nothing has been found at Kirkstead which can help to date it or identify its purpose and there are no records of anybody having dug for anything.

Perhaps tradition is not far out in identifying Kirkstead; the name may be a folk memory of ceremonies of religious significance being held there, a not unlikely supposition since the name 'kirk' has been given to prehistoric stone circles in Cumbria, for example, 'Sunken Kirk' at Swinside, Millom. That the Kirkstead is rectangular and not circular as most prehistoric religious monuments are could be due to Roman influence which, again, could bring us back to Ninian. Remembering that Ninian came among his own people, apparently to steer or bully them back on to the straight and narrow path of true Christianity, it is possible that Kirkstead and what went on there under the direction of local priests, several generations removed from the original evangelists, was found to come under the headings of 'ill-planted', 'ill-gathered' or 'ill-built'.

However, Kirkstead and its purpose remain a mystery, and there is also a mystery about a small circular enclosure of fellside stones out on the neck of land between Whiteoak and Floutern. It has been described as a pit-dwelling, but this wild outpost of the valley is not a typical site for such a place. It could have been a watching post when the defence of the valley was important, or a hermitage or cell where some early Christian teacher found the solitude he required for the quiet contemplation which reactivated evangelical zeal. But again, as with Kirkstead, nothing is certain.

Another of the valley's folk tales centres on Gatesgarth and Honister Pass, a story which has been written up several times and more often than not today dismissed as pure fabrication.

The story is that a party of the Border Graham clan raided Borrowdale and were ambushed by the dalesmen on their way out over Honister. In a bloody battle the leader of the Scots was killed, at which point the battle ended, the booty was restored to its rightful owners and the Scots were allowed to bury their dead. According to legend the young chief of the Grahams was buried on a mountain top, and Miss Annie Nelson, quoting her grandfather, Auld Ned, as authority on the matter, was certain that the burial place was the cairn on Hindscarth. Other casualties of the fight were buried where they fell, and Miss Nelson said she could remember two stones, flat in the ground by the roadside just above the second bridge up Honister, which marked their graves. The stones, Miss Nelson said, had some lettering on them, but the lettering was worn off long ago. No trace of these stones can be found today.

When the valley was more populous and pious, it had three churches, at Loweswater, at Buttermere, and at Rannerdale. The Rannerdale chapel has disappeared although its site is still visible among the trees at the end of Rannerdale. Buttermere's original church was indeed the smallest in England, being only 17 feet long.

The Buttermere chapel was served by 'readers' who were

also schoolmasters, and their superior, the Lorton curate, kept an eye on the affairs of the parish by officiating at three or four Buttermere services a year.

Buttermere allowed its reader twenty shillings per annum, but he was helped to survive on this meagre stipend by the 'incidentals' which included whittlegate. This meant that he was allowed to enter his 'whittle' or knife at the tables of his parishioners for a few days of each year, a system which ensured that he was adequately fed. That some country church folk looked rather cynically on the whittlegate system is shown in the local idiom which colourfully interpreted whittlegate as allowing the parson 'the run of his teeth'. If, as often happened, since whittlegate parsons were usually notorious trenchermen, the priest was slow to rise from the table and the victuals it held, he was considered in local dialect to be 'tethered by t' teeth'.

The Buttermere reader was also allowed annually a pair of 'clogg shoes', wood-soled, iron shod, and a 'harden sark', which was a shirt of hemp or coarse linen, so coarse that no master of men would wear one new so long as he could get one of his men to wear it for the first month 'by way of breaking it in'. The reader also had 'geuse gate', the right of pasturing his geese on the common land, and, by and large, he did not do so badly because he also got school pence for teaching the children, and could always make something extra by helping out the local farmers at harvest or clipping times.

Underpaid or not, the reader at Butermere had the usual jobs of church work to do, and he had to take care of the church property which, some time after 1571 included "a fair cup of silver" for Communion. This was after the Reformation during which the more ornamental chalices had been confiscated and melted down. The 'fair cup' and its paten was obviously kept for special occasions because Buttermere also had a set of pewter communion vessels. These were eventually hurled into the depths of Buttermere Lake to prevent their desecration by secular use when they were no longer required for sacramental purposes.

The Parochial Church Council of 1874 seem to have had no reservations on the secular uses to which their sixteenth-century cup and paten would be put, for they quite happily accepted the offer of the then Earl of Lonsdale, patron of the living, of a new communion set in exchange for what was termed at the time "an old two-handled cup and paten".

Down the valley Loweswater parishioners kept their "fair cup of silver", and for four centuries have taken Communion from the old chalice, preferring this tiny, simple, paper-thin cup of silver to the bigger, heavier and more elaborate chalice which has been given to the church. The Elizabethan Loweswater chalice, dated 1571-2, is only 6¼ inches high with a bowl $3\frac{1}{8}$ inches wide at the top, a simple engraved design on the bowl reminding that this cup belongs to a time when communion vessels could be 'fair' but were not allowed to be elaborate. The marks on the cup are plain: a stag's head for the maker's mark; a leopard's head crowned; a lion passant, and a small black-letter 'o'. The paten-cover which matches the cup has the maker's initials 'J.F.' instead of the stag's head mark.

The cup shared a mystery with the more famous communion cup at St Margaret's, Westminster, for they both had the stag's head mark of the silversmith who made them. Whose mark it was nobody seemed to know because all the records of the Goldsmith's Company were destroyed in the Great Fire of London. The marks on the Loweswater paten solved the mystery. As it is certain that the cup and paten were made by the same silversmith, it seems that although he put his mark on the cup, he put his initials on the paten, the 'J.F.' identifying him as John Freeman who was in business as early as 1551, the date of the Cup at St Margaret's, and as late as 1576, the date of another communion cup he made for the church at Woodford in Wiltshire. However, Loweswater seems to be the only possessor of a matching cup and paten-cover by this maker which makes them extremely valuable. When these facts, and an approximate valuation were revealed to the parish in 1970, cup and paten-cover were put into a bank vault at Cockermouth until the security arrangements at St Bartholomew's could be made adequate for the protection of this virtually priceless plate.

Loweswater has not always been so careful of its treasures. In 1884, when St Bartholomew's underwent a major restoration, the old bell was found to have one of its responds broken. The Parochial Church Council decided to replace it with a new one, and, seeking to help to defray the cost, sold the old one to a Maryport scrap merchant. There, almost at the lip of the smelting furnace, it was found and rescued by Canon H.D. Rawnsley of Keswick, who bore it, less in triumph than in sorrow, to Crosthwaite Church where it remained over eighty-five years as part of the attractions of that infinitely attractive church.

This bell is dated in the fourteenth century, and is one of the most important in the Diocese of Carlisle. It was not until 1969 that the successors of those uncaring dalesmen were allowed to have the bell back at Loweswater. It was repaired in 1972 and then resumed its original job of calling the dalesmen and women to worship.

Nothing of man's work in the valley is as old as the burial tumuli on the top of Carlin Knott and the two prehistoric villages, one on the flat land between the shore of Crummock and Scale Force and the other on Lanthwaite Green beside the turbulent Liza beck. Recently designated as an ancient monument, the village on Lanthwaite Green is roughly circular with a surrounding bank of cobbles. Inside are smaller cobble enclosures, perhaps the footings of huts or enclosures for animals. All that has been found there, in what must have been a quite casual examination, are a few 'pot-boilers' – stones which were heated in fires and then put into the pots to heat or cook the contents, a necessary method since there seem to have been no vessels capable of withstanding the direct heat of a fire.

Perhaps a systematic excavation of the Lanthwaite Green village would come up with some answers about the site, but, not unnaturally in such a situation, there is no great enthusiasm for digging the place up.

Old histories, Hutchinson among them, tell of a mysterious deposit of charcoal or cinder found under the topsoil in parts of the valley, attributing it to some holocaust which once swept the valley. This was, however, probably a relic of ancient industry, of charcoal burning or iron smelting.

At the foot of Lanthwaite Green is Cinderdale Common, and the name is explained by the existence beside the beck which flows off Lad Hows of traces of an old bloomery. Here iron ore was smelted with the aid of charcoal into 'blooms' of iron which could then be forged into tools and weapons. A few inches beneath the sod on Cinderdale Common can be found the ash and slag of this ancient industry which probably lasted as long as there was wood to burn into charcoal.

Of ancient agriculture there are, of course, many reminders. Most spectacular are the dry-stone walls which ramble up, down and across most of the fellsides and into places which prove that their builders were as nimble-footed as the Herdwick sheep. In Rannerdale, where this hidden valley broadens out to provide sufficient flat land for an ancient steading, there is a wall which almost qualifies as 'megalithic' from the size of its constituent stones. It crosses the flat and could have been intended as a defence work, or it could have been the work of industrious dalesmen doing two jobs at once in clearing the land of these huge boulders, and then using them to turn a slope into something approaching level ground.

On this level, or levelled, piece of land somebody once built a house which has now disappeared. Its site is still recognisable as a hump in the level ground where the spring which once supplied a family with water now turns a few square yards of ground into a perpetual swamp.

Rannerdale is one of the old routes into Buttermere from the West, and it provides one of Lakeland's greatest spring spectacles when acres of bluebells cover the floor of the dale, spreading up the slopes of Rannerdale Knotts and into the group of ancient crab apple trees and rowans which, in their own time, make an almost equally colourful contribution to the Rannerdale scene.

In the little offshoot vale which holds the Whiteoak beck is a remnant of bygone mining activities in an unfinished shaft. Further upstream the little beck takes a steep dive down a rock face into a deep pool at one of the real lonely places of the Lake Country where for years a pair of mistle thrushes nested at knee height in the fork of a rowan tree and pretended that human visitors did not exist.

Over the neck at the head of Whiteoak, past the cobble

circle of the 'pit dwelling' lonely Floutern Tarn is in view. Here at Floutern, as long as can be remembered, there has been a solitary heron which has found the fishing good. In Floutern, so the legend goes, swim some great black trout which, in true Lake Country tradition, are immortal. They prove the legend by refusing to take bait if an angler is prepared to walk up there and fish — and hope. The heron, not knowing the legend, stands patiently, silent and motionless in the dark shallows of the tarn waiting to stab like a striking snake at unwary minnows, and, when its crop is full, it flies slowly down Mosedale.

The Floutern Tarn heron could have been there for ever.

2

A Day To Remember

Several times in the history of Cumberland its inhabitants have strayed from the true faith. Towards the end of the fourth century there was St Ninian. In the middle of the sixth century, Kentigern, fleeing south from his persecutors in Strathclyde, was passing down the Eden Valley when he was told that the people among the mountains to the west had fallen away from the true faith and had turned to idolatry. Upon hearing this Kentigern swept through the Cumbrian mountains like an avenging angel and quickly returned the strays to the Christian fold in a campaign which is remembered today in the many churches which are dedicated to him in the district, Crosthwaite, Mungrisedale and Caldbeck among them.

If the Cumbrians of old had a penchant for raising their own gods, perhaps the habit has not entirely died out. Or so it seemed on October 23, 1954. On that day the inhabitants of Caldbeck, and about five thousand friends, honoured the memory of John Peel with a 'do' that will never be forgotten by anybody who was there.

It was the centenary of the death of the great Cumberland hunter whose fame still rings throughout the world in the song which starts:

"D'ye ken John Peel with his coat so gray,
D'ye ken John Peel at the break of day;
D'ye ken John Peel when he's far, far away
With his hounds and his horn in the morning?"

The centenary of a man's death should, perhaps, have been something of a solemn occasion, but it was not planned to be solemn, and it certainly did not turn out to be solemn. Far

26

from it. It was one of the noisiest, most boisterous and eventful days in Cumberland's history. It was also one of the wettest days anybody could remember, and this in a county which seems to have been given credit for inventing rain.

Typical of Cumbrians' non-conforming habits was the decision of the organisers to hold the 'do', not on November 13, the actual date of Peel's death, but on October 23. This was not because the promoters had decided that that this and any future marking of a Peel anniversary should, like Easter, be a moveable feast, but because this particular celebration simply had to be brought forward to bring it inside the hound trailing season, which ends on October 31. Nobody could imagine a Cumbrian festival on any scale being held without hound trails.

And so the John Peel Centenary was marked with fervour which would have done justice to a religious festival up to the point at which apparently limitless stocks of drink took over and focussed attention, and concentrated much of the action into the circus-sized beer tent thoughtfully provided by a local brewery.

Early in the morning there was a family occasion when fifty of John Peel's descendants gathered around his grave in Caldbeck Churchyard, and after a five-minute service a wreath was laid by Miss Joan Peel, of Bewaldeth, his oldest surviving relative.

Then the 'do' started. The rain began to fall, softly, as three packs of foxhounds met in the village and moved off in procession. In place of honour was the Blencathra Hunt because the 'Cathra calls itself the 'John Peel' pack, its hounds having some of Peel's hounds in their ancestry and because it hunts a lot of the old John Peel country. Then there was the Cumberland Hunt with joint Master, Mr C.N. de Courcy Parry, dressed in a hodden gray coat and beaver hat, and looking more like John Peel than Isaac Fawkes, who was supposed to represent Peel in the procession, and who wore an actual John Peel coat for the occasion.

The Cumberland Farmers' Foxhounds were also there, and so were the masters, the huntsmen, the whippers-in, and most of the followers of all the other Cumberland and West-morland fell foot-packs. There were some mounted followers who came with the Cumberland and the Cumberland Farmers hunts, most of them on horses the like of which John Peel never owned and seldom saw. He favoured the short, sturdy, but cleaned-limbed 'Galloway' which was equally at home on the low fells and the Solway Plain.

He rode to hounds in the low country, but used his horse purely as transport to fellside meets when he hunted on foot. It was to be remembered ever afterwards that Peel had his horses so well schooled in their duty of attending him in the unpredictabilities of fell foxhunting that they were usually waiting for him at the point at which he came back off the fell. The shape of the hounds in attendance would surprise Peel too because his hounds were leaner and somewhat smaller than hounds are today.

When he started hunting his own pack, after he had spent some time as huntsman to the private pack of Sir Frederick Fletcher Vane of Armathwaite Hall, Bassenthwaite, his hounds were a nondescript lot 'ratched together' from all arts and parts. These were augmented by gifts of hounds in singles and couples from local gentry, who ran their own packs, in appreciation of the fact that nobody could give followers a better hunt than John Peel.

Peel's innominate hunt gathered support as its reputation grew, but most of the support was in the form of followers and not in financial aid. Peel bore the expense himself from the income of his two little estates at Ruthwaite, where he lived and which had come to him on his marriage with Mary White, and Greenrigg at Caldbeck, which was his ancestral home.

Mostly Peel hunted the fells around Caldbeck, but a hunt could take him far outside what was regarded as his territory. He was not over-strict in hunt discipline when he was among the fells; it was unnecessary since most of the followers knew the game, and he was certainly no foxhunting purist in that he did not mind hunting a hare or a marten if there were no foxes about. Sometimes he went, by invitation, to hunt other country, and on these occasions hunt etiquette was strictly observed, especially at Brayton Hall where 'Old' Sir Wilfred Lawson always made it clear that his covers were to be fox-hunted only, and woe betide any young followers who defaulted by even looking at a hare.

The Caldbeck fells were the domain of the 'greyhound' fox, now probably extinct. This fox was lighter in colour, longer in the leg, stronger in the shoulder and perhaps a bit lighter in the brush than his lowland cousin, and the halcyon days of Peel and his friends were those spent in pursuit of such foxes. They had speed and stamina, and the hunts were long, fast and furious. Peel, who never spared his hounds, his horses or erring followers, was known on occasion to leave a hard-run fox to run another day and 'to keep the breed'.

When Peel's hounds were in full cry and 'varra nar fleein'' after a good fox all else could be forgotten — family, farm and all those other attachments of normal men.

To say that Peel was a keen hunter would be understating the case; he was a fanatic; he hunted with a fervour and urgency which was infectious. Once committed, men would go to any lengths to follow him, to try and match him in the field, mostly without success.

Always an early starter, Peel was often away before daybreak, and the repetition of the 'morning' theme in Graves's song emphasises this. Often the hunt's business for the day was over while the day was still young, but there were epic hunts which lasted through all the daylight hours and sometimes into the dark as well. Runs of 40, 60, even 80 miles were recorded which had Peel's pack of a dozen couple of hounds reduced to the last gallant and persistent two or three whose names, as a consequence, have been handed down with that of their master.

Britain was John Peel's favourite hound. He had many Britains because the name was handed down but the Britain which was particularly favoured by the great hunter was described by his eldest son, John — who, incidentally was known as 'Young' John Peel right up to his death at the age of 92. The best of the Britains was probably a late-comer because it received no mention in Graves's song. But Ruby, Ranter, Royal and Bellmen were also favourite hounds in their time, and they did earn a mention in the song. The other names in Peel's pack were Burthwaite, Bowler, Charmer, Crafty, Delly, Dancer, Drunkard, Glory, Leader, Lifter, Lucy, Lilter, Lively, Lofty, Melody, Merry, Stormy,

Towler and Welcome, and these are names still handed down in the foxhound packs which hunt the Cumberland fells.

Much has been made of Peel as a 'running huntsman', meaning that he mostly followed his hounds on foot, but the fact that he always wore at least one spur shows that he rode too. He rode horses as a matter of course about his work as a practical farmer; he rode to market; he was a bit of a horse trader because that occupation ran in the family. The greatest hunts he had were on horseback.

His favourite pony was called 'Dunny', a nag, according to Young John Peel interviewed in 1886, 'of neah great breeding,' and, taken all round, of no great beauty either. Dunny stood at 14.3 hands, and had extraordinary endurance. It would, again according to Young John, "walk or creep, slidder down or cropple up wherever a man could, and would stand for a week for owder me fadder or me".

John Peel rode his horse with judgment because he never knew how long a chase would last, and since he had many which lasted all day, laid great store on preserving the energy of his steed, and he taught Young John to do the same.

"We minded t' whip", said Young John, the aim being to try and conserve the horse's energy in order to be up with the hounds and in at the kill. But when a straight-necked fox had the hounds in full cry after him, nobody ever rode straighter or more fearlessly than John Peel and his son.

> I've followed John Peel both often and far
> O'er the rasper fence, the gate and the bar.

And over dry-stone walls, backs and ghylls, and such rough ground that some men would never dream of leading a horse over it, much less riding it.

Long hunts; tiring, exciting days, narrow escapes; the wiles of the fox and the strength of the hounds were recounted in the nearest hostelry when the hunts were over. If the Ellen, the Caldew, the Cocker or the Derwent, or even the Eden were in the line of the hunt, they were jumped, crossed or run into, and both old John Peel and John Peel the Younger often had to struggle to get to the other side, sometimes horse and man landing at different places after a particularly rough crossing of a swollen river.

In his ninetieth year, Young John remembered a hunt with his father which started at the Isel covers with thirty-three mounted followers. It was such a gruelling, exciting chase, with so many horses winded, abandoned and borrowed, that at the end there was not a man, among those who finished, who was riding the horse he started with.

It was January, 1848, and to make sure that the fox, when found, would move away, young Peel and a few more had spent the previous evening stopping up earths and badger setts and anything else in which a fox might find refuge.

Shortly after daybreak the riders and the foot followers — for nobody knew whether a hunt would turn towards the fell or lowland — waited around the covers listening for sounds from the hounds that a fox had been found. A whimper came, a single bellow, and then the chorus of the pack as they rattled a fox round inside the covers three times before breaking.

When it broke cover, followers jammed their hats tight on and set off in pursuit. Three times they galloped over The Hay, and three times they came back again. The fourth time, the riders were viewing the fox, brush streaming behind him straight as a stick, and the hounds with their heads up because they could now see the quarry.

Wythop Woods, thick with undergrowth, was given to the hounds and fox while the riders waited for another break from cover. The hounds continued to give mouth from the depths of the wood as they circled after their prey, keeping the riders on tenterhooks to try and anticipate the direction of the break.

When it came out, the fox headed for Bassenthwaite Head, and Dodd and Skiddaw breast were all passed as the fox headed for Stockdale Head, running straight as a die now with no signs of tiring.

There were covers nearby, but hounds were too close and the fox, passing Overwater Tarn, tried to baffle his pursuers by getting among some freshly-salved sheep which exploded to all corners of the field at the intrusion. He almost succeeded because sheep-salve is an all-pervading scent even to the human nostril, let alone the finely tuned organs of a pack of hounds.

The sheep caused a check, but Young John Peel, well up

with the hounds in company with his father, dismounted to put his beauties to rights, halloahed them together and soon had them running, heads up and giving mouth with every stride.

Young John had given his father his horse to lead, and as soon as the hounds got away again the old man threw himself off his horse, now utterly spent, and mounted his son's horse, shouting "Here! Thoo can tak mine," and set off in pursuit.

With old John was Nicholson, of Broughton who had ridden up in the meantime, and Young John was left with a thoroughly winded horse and most of the day still ahead of him. He never thought of complaining.

Over the fell between Ruthwaite and Ireby the hunt raced on, and at this point gained a recruit. Robinson Bell, of the Sun Inn, Ireby, a son-in-law of John Peel, was going out to cart turnips with 'blinder, braffin and bridle' on his cart horse, but when he heard the hounds he threw off collar, blinkers and other gear and mounted bareback to follow.

The newcomer on a fresh horse was noticed by Faulder of Cockermouth, who came galloping up and offered Robinson ten shillings for the use of his nag "an' deu what thoo likes wid mine," but was refused.

At Snittlegarth, Robinson Bell, conscious now of the discomfort of bareback riding, found himself a 'cuddy pad' to make things easier, and at the same place Cape of Cockermouth had to lead his horse staggering into the stable.

The hunt continued. Over Whitrigg and Borrowscale Hill before turning down for Bothel, and between that village and Threapland, beside the lime kilns, the fox turned for Aspatria Town End to head for Brayton where, at the front door of the Hall, he was pulled down.

Robinson Bell was first up and seized the fox, and next was Nicholson, now riding old John Peel's horse which had had its second wind. How he got hold of it nobody seems to know.

Golightly of Bewaldeth was given the brush being considered entitled to it for keeping well up from the find to the kill, and old John Peel offered the mask to Sir Wilfred Lawson, naturally enough because the hunt both started and finished on Lawson ground.

Crab apples and mountain ash add to the beauty of the spring scene
in Rannerdale

Loweswater from Water End (from a nineteenth-century drawing
by Thomas Allom)

A latter-day John Peel. Mr C. N. de Courcy Parry (*left*) in period garb at the start of the hunt which marked the John Peel centenary. His mount, 'Badger', spiked when leaping a fence, was the day's only casualty

According to map distances, this was a run of about 60 miles, and those who took part never stopped talking about it because the hounds ran unchecked all the way except when the fox sought to throw them by getting among the salved sheep at Overwater.

At that time, old John was 72 years old and Young John was 51.

Caldbeck's preparations to mark the centenary of John Peel's death took into account the fact that the celebration would be more than a purely village affair.

Half a ton of potatoes were peeled, carcases of mutton were cut up and stones of onions peeled for 'tatie pots'. There was no question as to what the visitors would be offered; it was tatie pot all the way, each with a black pudding on top, and served with pickled onion and pickled red cabbage. Nearly every oven in Caldbeck had a tatie-pot in it, and the smell spread through the village, a welcoming, appetising aroma on such a miserable wet day.

When the day had dawned, darkly cold and threatening rain, it was feared that the weather would spoil everything, that the people who were expected would stay away. Their fears took no account of John Peel fervour which, it became apparent as the day wore on, had an almost hypnotic effect.

Slow processions of traffic moved along the roads over Caldbeck Moor where the little Herdwick sheep cropped the grass oblivious of either the excitement or the weather; where the little wild black fell ponies gathered in groups seeking what shelter they could get in folds in the ground. They came in past Park End where Peel was born, and through Ruthwaite on the banks of the River Ellen, where he died, and the nearer they got to Caldbeck the greater became the traffic congestion.

Most people there that day visited John Peel's grave in the parish churchyard, beating into a muddy smear the bright green path that had been trodden there on less crowded occasions, the headstone brightly painted gleaming white, the lettering in black recording the life spans of John and Mary, and some of their family including 'Young' John.

Some of the visitors went into St Kentigern's Church, and

a few sat in the front pew on the right where John waited for his bride when parental blessing had finally been given to their union.

Perhaps they expected an echo of that earlier occasion when the impetuous John and willing Mary had had their banns called for the first time before a thunderstruck congregation. John and Mary had handed their names in to the parson, asking for the banns to be called, and he never considered checking with the parents of the young couple.

"If anybody knows any just cause or impediment . . . " droned Parson Lynn, and the mother of the bride-to-be rose in her seat and declared for all to hear, "They're far ower young," which was considered impediment enough, for there was no second time of asking of these banns of marriage.

A believer in the saying, "Happy is the wooing that's not long a-doing", John refused to wait and took off with Mary for Gretna Green on his father's best horse, and broke the news of his wedding there with an exhuberant "View Halloo" as they rode back into Caldbeck.

John's father, William Peel, was a horse trader, and, according to Richard Greenup of Caldbeck, "a varra honest and honourable yen". When he sold an animal, he did so with the equivalent of the modern guarantee because he allowed a reasonable time for the horse to be tried, and if it was not satisfactory, he would take it back. This was fair trading indeed in a time when horse deals were 'sharp' and horse dealers were regarded with almost universal suspicion.

With John and Mary back from Gretna Green, married in the eyes of the law, Mary's parents had to relent and give their blessing. But not on a Gretna Green marriage. Mrs White insisted upon a proper church wedding, and so John and Mary stood before the altar at St Kentigern's on December 18, 1797. Wishing nothing but the best for her daughter, Mrs White hoped the Rector would perform the ceremony, but he was away, and his curate, Joseph Rogerson, officiated.

Mary bore John thirteen children, and twelve of them survived into adulthood, the odd one being Jonathan who died at the age of two. The weakling of the family was Peter, said to be 'dwarfish and imperfect', who died at the age of 27. For Peter, Peel had a special affection which was missing from his relationships with the rest of his family, and with Peter, John would spend hours recounting details of his hunts. Peel went hunting while Peter lay dead at home, and when he became aware of chuntering in the village at his lack of respect for his own dead he answered by putting the brush of the newly-caught fox in the coffin beside his son.

On that November day in 1840, John Peel with his dozen couple of hounds had more success than the three packs which met to celebrate in Caldbeck 114 years later. None of the three packs registered a kill, and a damper was put on the proceedings when word came back that Mr de Courcy Parry's hunter 'Badger' had been spiked by a stake when jumping a fence and had to be destroyed.

But the celebrations went on. Tatie-pots, steaming through the snow-white cloths which protected them from the rain, were carried from cottages to the village hall where the women dishing it up lost count of the number of sittings they had served.

Lectures on old times and exhibitions of bygones drew people thankfully in out of the rain, and in the school all the descendants of John Peel known to be present were gathered together for a commemmorative photograph, the youngest Peel of all testing newly-emerging teeth on the rim of an authentic John Peel hunting horn for the benefit of the *Daily Express*. Everybody who could was proud to claim descent from this mighty Nimrod John Peel; his posterity always forebore to criticise, to join in the criticism which was levelled at him for allegedly neglecting his family by spending too much of his time and coin on his hunting.

In all that has been recorded of the life and times of John Peel, there is only one mention of his having impoverished himself through his hunting, and that reference is made by John Woodcock Graves, author of the words of the song, in his autobiographical notes to his contributions to Gilpin's *Songs and Ballads of Cumberland*.

Peel was as generous as every true sportsman ever must be. He was free with the glass 'at the heel of the hunt'; but a better heart never throbbed in man. His honour was never once questioned in his lifetime.

In the latter part of his life his estate was embarrassed, but the right sort in all Cumberland called a meet some years since, and before parting they sang 'John Peel' in full chorus, closing by presenting him with a handsome gratuity which empowered him to shake off his encumbrances, and die with a 'hark tally-ho.'

Graves wrote this in or about 1865, eleven years after Peel's death and thirty-two years after he had himself emigrated to Tasmania. However, Peel's family hotly denied that he ever became financially embarrassed because of the money he spent on hunting, his principal defenders being Young John, who was interviewed a year before his death in 1887, and his son-in-law Robinson Bell, of Ireby, who insisted that Peel never got any assistance from the neighbouring gentry who followed his hounds.

Peel is never heard doing much about his farm, but it is as a hunter, not a farmer, that he is remembered. And with six sons to his name, and six daughters, there were plenty of hands available, sufficient even to allow the eldest, young John, to spend as many days hunting as his father.

John Peel was far from being the perfect man, the perfect husband, father, farmer or anything else. He did what he wanted to do and used all his means physical and financial to do it well. That he did it better than anybody else in his time is history.

If John Peel escaped from home and family responsibilities in his hunting; got away from the realities of a far-from-easy life, then he also provided a means of escape for others who were more tightly shackled to their responsibilities. When Peel's hounds were around, farmers dropped what they were doing and joined in the hunt; boys played truant from school to follow him, and often found the schoolmaster alongside them in the field.

In the beer tent, the drinkers, drowning the memory of John Peel with the sort of dedication Irishmen reserve for the shamrock on St Patrick's Day, splashed happily around in ankle-deep mud, talking louder, laughing longer as the day wore on.

There was a competition for singing the best hunting song, but voices that could rattle the rafters of the Kirkstile Inn at Loweswater were almost inaudible against the babble of voices and the tinkle of cash registers, besides which the songs were lost for an echo against the sagging canvas of the big tent. There was that other peculiarly Cumbrian pastime of 'gurning through a braffin' which involved making funny faces through a horse collar. Men with shotguns blasted away at clay pigeons and hit some of them; children raced for prizes wearing Wellington boots which upset the form by which the handicapper worked.

Only the men selling milk shakes in a tent on the semi-deserted sports field had a poor day because milk simply did not seem to be the drink to fit the occasion — or the weather.

People stood, dripping, in the pouring rain outside the house in Midtown where John Woodcock Graves lived, and where he wrote the song which, more than foxhunting, won fame for John Peel.

The song was written in 1829 when Peel and Graves were relaxing after a day's hunting, and making arrangements for the next meet.

It was written to the music of an old Border tune called "Bonnie (or Canny) Annie". At the start, it was in Cumberland dialect, which Graves later anglicised, and then the original, borrowed tune, was worked upon by William Metcalfe, a bass singer at Carlisle Cathedral and given a good send-off at a dinner of the Cumberland Benevolent Association in London. It was an immediate success.

The fame of John Peel spread as the song became popular, and though Cumberland had other great hunters, none acquired more than a purely local fame. Other writers wrote of other hunters, and others set them to music, or, as Graves had done, borrowed other old tunes, but none achieved the popularity of "D'ye ken John Peel?"

This hunters' song is the Cumberland anthem, and the march of the old county regiment, the Border Regiment. It was heard at the relief of Lucknow, and, it is said, the men of the 34th Foot (predecessors of the Border Regiment) whistled it as they serviced the cavalrymen of the Light Brigade before they charged the Russian guns at Balaclava the year John Peel died.

John Peel died at Ruthwaite, aged 78. Three thousand

people came to the funeral at Caldbeck, more than had ever
been to a funeral there. That was a true measure of his fame
as a hunter; the song had not yet made much impact.

He is Caldbeck's most famous son. He fills a vacuum
because Caldbeck has no stately home and has had no stately
families to make its history, except a family of Vaux, of
Greenrigg, who claimed to have come over with the Con-
queror and had fourteen generations of the family recorded
as buried in the parish churchyard.

The rain continued, and people still walked about
Caldbeck with rapt expressions. The action was still mainly in
the beer tent where there was a competition for blowing
hunting horns. Some fine, soaring calls were sounded, but
they tailed off into dispirited spits and gurgles as the day
wore on. Such was the dedication of the contestants that the
hunting horns were never entirely silent, not even when a
contestant tripped over somebody's foot. He continued to
blow whilst stretched out full length in the mud.

Graves wrote that "Peel's 'View Halloa' would awaken the
dead", but John Peel and his family, and the rest of the
village forefathers slept on in the parish churchyard.

So John Peel was remembered by the wettest, muddiest,
perhaps the happiest throng ever to grace a Cumberland
occasion. The real magic of the day lay in the fact that even
those who were not attracted to the beer tent saw the day
out in rain which never stopped. Newspaper reports of that
occasion state that the thousands who went to Caldbeck
'braved' the rain, but, truth to tell, most of them did not
seem to notice it was raining, and a large number of people
walked about the straggling village of Caldbeck that day with
the sort of look on their faces which belongs more to pilgrims
at Mecca or to the Holy Sepulchre than to people remembering that a farmer-hunter had died a hundred years ago.

3

The Singer of the Song

"By Jove, Peel, you'll be sung when we're both run to earth."

These words, immortal, like the words of the song John Woodcock Graves had just written when he said them, are found in every account which has been written about the birth of the famous hunting song "in a snug parlour at Caldbeck."

Peel was 'run to earth' in 1854; Graves outlived him by thirty-two years and died in Tasmania. In the Valhalla to which hunters go, John Woodcock Graves is probably quite happy that the posthumous fame is mainly Peel's. He intended it that way.

Graves can never be forgotten as long as the song is sung; but, apart from "D'ye ken John Peel?" he did nothing in his life that is memorable; he did not strive for popularity and he earned very little of it; he lost more friends than he made. He was a great loser all his life. He was not, like the great majority of his time when wealth was confined to the comparative few, a born loser, but he worked at it. He lost money on almost everything he touched. His failures were not spectacular because he did not lose sufficient money to deserve that description. But he was consistent: he was one of the most consistent failures ever to win even a modicum of public notice.

And his one great triumph, his immortal song, did not make John Woodcock Graves a single penny.

Graves was born at Wigton, the only son of an ironmonger who died when John was a boy, leaving behind him a financial mess, a widow, several daughters and the only son. If a key is sought to John Woodcock Graves' misspent life it must be that he was an only son. He seems to have been thoroughly spoiled ('wasted', as they would say in Wigton at

39

the time) by his mother, and indulged in some extent by uncles and aunts.

'Nanny' Graves, as his mother was called by most who knew her in Wigton, had ideas for her family which her acquaintances believed were above their station in life, and to this end she cherished the 'Jerome Mantle', the christening robe of a Count Jerome de Salis, which was given to her by a relative who married a refugee French nobleman at the time of the French Revolution.

John and his sisters all wore the Jerome Mantle at their christening, a fact which was pointed out to all who cared to listen. Perhaps Nanny Graves hoped the mantle would bring the family some good luck.

John was sent for his education to Cockermouth Grammar School which had had such illustrious old boys as William Wordsworth and Fletcher Christian. He was nine years old, and had completed three years' schooling when his father died, and his schooling was continued in "a clay daubin in a backyard" in Wigton.

At the age of fourteen John was back in Cockermouth with his Uncle George, house, sign and coach painter, evidently to learn the trade and hopefully, since his uncle and aunt had no children of their own, to inherit the business.

"He rarely taught me anything," Graves was to recall. At any rate, he learned something about painting, sufficient to implant in the mind of young John the idea of becoming an artist.

John appears to have had a great deal of freedom at Cockermouth because his uncle and aunt had a second string to their commercial bow in a bathing hotel at Skinburness which occupied a great deal of their time.

With time on his hands, he developed a love of hunting and frequently followed the hounds of Joseph Steel, of Wood Hall, Cockermouth, almost certainly on foot because this was foot-pack country, and because Graves never wrote or said anything which indicated that he had any fondness at all for horses or riding.

In Cockermouth John found a friend in Joseph Falder, an old bachelor who lived with his sister. "To that man," Graves wrote, "I owe anything good that I have done or know. He lived a hundred years too soon. He was John Dalton's intimate friend; and I could pourtray them shaking hands, such a thrilling effect did their meeting produce on my young mind . . . Dear amiable Jo Falder! He fixed in me a love of Truth, and bent my purpose to pursue it, guarding me against having my mind weakened by the false theories of superstitions which would inevitably arise around my walk in life."[1]

Graves several times met the renowned mathematician, Dalton, who must have been in marked contrast to "dear amiable Jo": a successful man who had won wide renown, and the simple homespun philosopher whose life and ambitions were fulfilled in a Cockermouth cottage.[2]

Uncle George gave up his business in Cockermouth to give more attention to the bathing hotel at Skinburness, and John married Jane Atkinson of Rosley, and took up residence on Market Hill, Wigton, but his wife died within the year.

Graves' financial arrangements at that time are a mystery. Whether his wife had brought him a bit of money, or whether he was receiving funds from his uncle and aunt is not known. In his short autobiography he made no mention of having employment, but somehow he was able in the next five years to spend his time "in the acquirement of knowledge through reading, study and experimenting, in company with Walter Simpson, a very superior young man". He makes it appear that he was concerned in almost anything that had nothing to do with making a living, but we only have his word for it.

In 1820 he married Abigail Porthouse whom he had known since childhood — "the fatal sell of my life", he was to call the marriage later, which was less than just to the statuesque and very capable Abigail who not only bore him eight children but raised six of them, without much help or encouragement from their father.

They lived at Caldbeck, in Gate House, opposite the smithy in Midtown, and he set up a wool weaving industry in partnership with Edward Scott. He made a wreck of this partly because of his quarrels with his partner, partly because he often absented himself foxhunting with John Peel, and partly because he committed what little capital he had into a get-rich-quick coal-mining scheme on the Scottish Border.

The coal mine failed; his woollen mill languished, he quarelled with friends, and in a temper decided to emigrate.

In the meantime, he had written "D'ye ken John Peel?" in the parlour of his home, and at the time of his leaving for Tasmania, it was just another of a number of hunting songs, not very tuneful, not every singable, in the repertoire of after-hunt songsters in the local inn.

He left the mill, machinery, book debts etc. in the hands of a relative to provide for the two daughters he left behind, and landed in Hobart Town, Tasmania, on August 26, 1833. With Graves and Abigail were four children, and an Irish servant, Mary Foy, who refused to leave them because she adored Mrs Graves.

Two of Graves' children probably died in infancy; the two daughters he left at home disappear from the story. The four who lived through the trials and tribulations of life with father in Tasmania were John Woodcock junior, Mary Amnie, Joseph, and another daughter, Isabella.

In Hobart, Graves, now forty-five years of age and in the full vigour of his manhood, again tried the wool-milling business, and, true to form, failed at it again.

By his own account, Graves landed at Hobart with only ten pounds in his pocket, but the family possessions also included some valuable pictures, the Jerome Mantle, some books, and many gifts which had been made to Abigail on her marriage. The provident Abigail had also laid in a stock of three years' clothing for each of them.

Hobart was a penal settlement, and the convicts had a modicum of freedom which was proved when one of them broke into the Graves house the first night they were there, making off with some of their meagre possessions. When the alarm was raised, Graves set off after the thief and caught him after a two-mile chase.

It was an experience which could have put them off convicts for the rest of their lives, but not long afterwards they were inviting convicts into their home to share their meals. Special convicts these: Cumberland men who had been transported for what, even then, seemed minor crimes.

Graves's sympathies with the convicts; his criticism of the cruelty of the authorities — the slightest offence was punishable by a severe flogging – did not escape notice. It was not his intention that they should, for he wrote letters to the local newspaper stating his point of view.

Then he had a row with the authorities for their failure to allot him a piece of land of the size promised to immigrants, and another lot of letters were written and sent off. From his lofty standpoint, Graves could not conceive of his being wrong about anything, and when his letters went beyond being a nuisance to those in authority at Hobart, and began to utter threats, the authorities took appropriate action. They had him locked up in a lunatic asylum from which he escaped.

There can be little doubt that Graves was a misfit in Tasmania. He refused to put his mind or his hands to anything constructive which set him apart from the rest of the colonists who were building their new world with the sweat of their brows. Out of sorts with himself and everybody else, Graves often took it out on his family; had rows with his wife and found vent for pent-up rages by beating his children. His daughter, Mary Amnie later recalled these floggings with the birch which became a regular feature of life with John Woodcock Graves. The worst sufferer was John Woodcock junior who had a thigh-bone damaged in one of these floggings, and was confined to bed for three years. He was cripped for life.

The family no doubt welcomed those times when the head of the household, following the age-old custom of the aboriginal inhabitants, went 'walkabout'. But whereas the walkabouts of the aborigines were purely instinctive and seasonal, John's were in search of a new life, new scenes, to get away from his wife, and irregular in duration.

While rambling from one colony to another in Tasmania and the Australian mainland, Graves occupied his mind on mechanical inventions and proved more than once that his mind was truly inventive. He also spent a great deal of time trying to discover perpetual motion.

The most memorable of his walkabouts lasted three years. It was particularly memorable in the family home In Hobart because Graves had made absolutely no provision for the maintenance of his family. Abigail kept her children fed by teaching at the Government school from nine till four, and then teaching music and drawing at another school from four till six, all the time insisting that her children should attend to their schooling.

Gradually she sold her few treasures to buy food and clothing until all that was left was the Jerome Mantle. It was sold one winter night. The Jerome Mantle was made of cream-coloured satin "very thick, lined with rich cream silk, and had a massive ring of cream silk ten inches deep" — the description given later in life by Mary Amnie whose job it was to sell the mantle. "My mother folded it in a towel and gave it to me to take to a kind-hearted woman who had come out with us. I carried the message to the woman to send for the mantle what she thought fit. I took back to my mother a packet of tea."

At length the family had to split up. Abigail had to accept an offer from Dr (later Sir Robert) Officier of a post as matron of the Queen's Orphan Asylum. She was allowed to take the crippled John Woodcock junior with her. Mary Amnie went to a doctor's home in New Norfolk to teach three children "and be treated as one of the family — without pay". The younger boy Joseph was sent off to school, but being of an independent and practical turn of mind, decided that he would not be a burden on his mother for school fees, and ran away. He got a job in a shipwright's yard on the river Derwent, and, by hard work, prospered in the timber business. Isabella was taken by the Bishop of Tasmania into his household, but obviously not as a servant because she was to make a very good marriage.

When Graves returned home from his long walkabout and found the home broken up and the family scattered, he was angry, but by now Abigail was used to his tempers and refused to set up home again for her wandering spouse.

It was probably after this that Graves and Abigail separated for good, for there is no indication that they ever lived together again. Abigail died in 1858, Graves reported in a footnote to his autobiography, adding "God be thanked for His mercy!"

His sentiments were not shared by his children who were devoted to their mother, but who, nontheless retained some

respect for their father, and, later, attended — even
pandered — to his wants.

In the care of his mother at the orphanage. John
Woodcock junior, although crippled, studied hard. When he
was sent off to boarding school he found lodging in some
casks on a wharf rather than allow his mother to pay for his
board and lodging. Of the worst days of the Graves family in
Tasmania, Mary Amnie wrote: 'The whole of our family had
a great dread of letting anybody know that we were poor. We
were content with what we had; our wants were our own
secrets."

When John Woodcock junior finally passed his examin-
ations and qualified as a barrister, a newspaper arrived with
the results. Abigail scanned the column and then, in her
relief, lapsed into the broadest of Cumberland dialects (which
neither she nor her husband ever lost) and said: "Sista, here
oor Jwohn's neame at t' heed o' t' list."

By now John Peel was becoming more than a pleasant
interlude in the memory of John Woodcock Graves. The song
had become popular, and Graves began to bask a little in the
glory he had attained, albeit in a small measure, and with no
pecuniary benefit to himself.

When young John Woodcock became a rich man, he kept
racehorses and named one of them 'John Peel'. He also made
his father an allowance which allowed John senior to give
more time to his inventions. He did not succeed in inventing
anything at this stage, frequently finding that the things he
invented had already been invented by somebody else, a state
of affairs which prompted him to write: "I have always made
a point of smashing my best work whenever I have found my
ideas forestalled. I hate the man who apes the manners and
habits of another."

Graves was now as happy as he had ever been, proud of his
eldest son "as good a sportsman as ever handled a gun", and
of Joseph whose fortune Graves estimated at a hundred
thousand pounds; of Mary Amnie who had married a
Melbourne journalist called Hubbard; of Isabella whose
husband was the Treasurer-General of Cape Colony.

When John Woodcock junior died at the age of 41 the
news was conveyed to his father by Mary Amnie Hubbard.

"My first salute was from a lovely thoroughbred greyhound, commencing with a dubious growl," she wrote. "I returned her salutation with 'Good lass; here, my pet.' and as we Graves have all the same voice, she knew as once I was one of the household, and came to me fawning and wagging her tail . . . and there my father sat in front of a large fire, a table close by covered with books, instruments, minerals, acids, triangles, squares, and all kinds of mathematical instruments. He turned his head for a moment and said: 'Hey, Amnie, is that thee?' "

Realising that new arrangements would now have to be made for the care of her father, Mary Amnie had the idea of providing another home for him.

When Mary Amnie suggested that they should provide Graves with a small cottage in which to end his days, Joseph put his foot down. "No!" he said emphatically. "I know father. If he had a house at the top of Mount Wellington he would want it at the bottom. If he had it at the bottom, he would want it at the top. If in the East he would want it in the West. I will do nothing about the cottage, but I will provide for him liberally in every sense of the word, and he may do as he will with it."

So Mary Amnie herself spent four hundred pounds on a cottage for her father. She made accommodation for a housekeeper — whose services Graves refused because he would have no truck with any woman but his daughter.

But Graves was, even at this late stage in his life, not a settling sort. He tired of this sheltered, secluded life, and one day Mary Amnie found he had abandoned his cottage. She ran him to earth in a back room in a back street in Hobart, anxious that she should sell the cottage and give him the money for some new wild scheme he had in view. She owed the bank one hundred pounds on the house, and so she sold it.

His family continued to help him financially, but gave up all efforts to settle him down.

Graves kept in regular correspondence with old friends in Cumberland, and his letters may have suggested (though Graves strenuously denied it) that his circumstances had become straitened. His song had now become a world-wide hit, and his Cumberland friends, knowing that Graves had not made a penny out of it, got together a subscription and raised one hundred pounds for him. Graves's reaction to this came in a letter to Edward Wilson of Mealsgate, saying that he was tenderly touched by the solicitude of his friends, but that it was a mistake to say that he was 'on the rocks'. When the generators of the subscription decided that the money would be sent to him at the rate of twenty pounds a year, however, Graves countered by complaining at the 'pauper-like doles', and requesting that he should be sent the entire sum.

Graves seems to have written most of his life, but to have published only a little. His song won him fame enough to be featured in *Songs and Ballads of Cumberland* edited by Sidney Gilpin in 1865. Included were his "D'ye ken John Peel?" and five other poems and the biographical piece always regarded as his 'official' autobiography.

One of the poems was his "Monody on John Peel", which he wrote on hearing of the death of the hunter and which was first published in the *Wigton Advertiser*:

> Each hound gave a howl and last look at the horn,
> (Who saith that a dog cannot feel?)
> Then singled to pine, all dejected, forlorn,
> And died on the death of John Peel.

Living in his dream world of achieving greatness by his inventions; wrapped around with nostalgia for old remembered faces and places, John Woodcock Graves could still write a poem which caught the fancy of Cumbrians at home.

His letters to friends in Cumberland were eagerly read, and pounced upon for publication in the local newspapers. Some were kept as mementoes of the writer of the song — to some effect in the case of one letter which was sold recently for one hundred pounds.

Occasionally he was sent a local newspaper, if the sender thought there anything of interest for the exile. In 1876 a correspondent to the *West Cumberland Times* told the story about Askew Peel (John Peel's Brother) and a horse deal which was written in dialect and signed "J.W.G. Raves".

By December the Editor of the *West Cumberland Times*

had a letter from Graves:

"From Cockermouth", I exclaimed, in ecstasy, and fell on it as old Ruby at a finish. A glance in it stayed me at a letter in the dialect marked for me, which I read aloud to two friends in glee, but was disappointed by their asking, "What the devil is it all about?" However, they had praise when I Anglicised it. I then took it to my studio, and laying it before me alone, fell into reading backwards on a long life, as scrambling among the tombs of memory. O that gem of the mental faculties!

Here I was for a moment sad, for very lately I have been alarmed at finding it fail, although I have not a pain or a scratch, and I daily hear, "Lo Mr Graves, you are a wonderful man," while I cannot hear of one of my age in these colonies to mentally and physically cope with me . . .

Busy inventing, I am heedless of condition individually, and my family being all ensconced in abundance, and throwing off swarms, they buzz around; while I am ever in abstruse studies of my own —my own mathematics and mechanics, read out of nature.

Of late years I have regretted much at mis-spent time and means, and mourned at the lack of early tuition in anything. Yet, again, I claim courage to become artist, editor, or anything and everything, and condole over a hale mind and body, breathed into me in joyous boyhood after the hounds over the Embleton fells.

It is eventide and late, while I find I am manifesting 'narrative age' or tumbling into egotism; but while I write of, or to, Cockermouth; while I reflect on the inestimable mentor of my dawning vision, I could bound to him, and, weeping yet cry, "My dearest Jo Falder you are not dead, nor ever can die. Give me that lean, meagre, but ever welcome hand, as I had it last, once more, and let me die for you."

A regular correspondent, William Hannah, of Stanthwaite, Uldale wrote that the style of Graves's letters was "characteristic of the true-born Cumbrian — almost rising to the sublime, almost descending to the comic — in fact that everlasting egotism is so firmly established in the Cumberland cranium that neither years, change of diet nor change of climate can alter it."

That Graves lived not entirely in obscurity in his adopted land is shown in an extract from the Hobart Mercury on May 26, 1882, reporting an election;

Among others who issued from the booth after having done their duty as 'free and independent electors' was a very old man, bent with age, and carrying a bundle tied up in a red pocket handkerchief.

Sole survivor? An example of the 'greyhound' fox hunted by John Peel—in fact, it is claimed that this was one of John's kills. The species is now extinct; this one is stuffed

Never did a bigger crowd see the start of a hunt in Cumberland. Some of the followers of the John Peel Centenary hunt

The man himself . . .
the only photograph
ever taken of the hunter,
John Peel

In old age:
John Woodcock Graves
(from a photograph)

He spoke to no-one but walked quietly up the street. He was the author of the famous sporting song 'D'ye ken John Peel?' It has been the song of the hunter, and been chanted round many a well-furnished board in the days of port wine drinking fox-hunting squires. There are few of the old school of sportsmen who, 30 or 40 years ago followed the hounds, but will remember the song, and perhaps some inquisitive youth may ask one 'Who wrote it?' In all probability the answer will be 'Oh, heaven knows; I don't. Some poor devil of a literary fellow, I suppose.'

And so old John Woodcock Graves has tasted of fame, and found it, like Dead-sea apples, peculiarly unprofitable.

When Graves was taken with his final illness, he was sure he would recover, and would not let the ever attentive Mary Amnie stay with him. She recorded:

To the last he was sternly independent, proud as Lucifer, and just as violent as ever he was when a young man. He must have been very handsome in his youth. His figure was simply perfect. I think the hunting field did a great deal towards making him what he was physically. His lungs were as sound as a bell, and to the last he was master.

I know the spot where he rests, after the turbulent storm of life through which he has passed; and as I reflect, what a wasted life it has been! A total shipwreck made of what might have been all goodness and greatness in man — poor father!

He lies on a beautiful hill in a small bay, on the margin of the river Derwent. The ground is about an hour's easy walk from Hobart Town; and in days gone by father used to take us for a stroll in the early morning far beyond it to the beautiful gardens and orchards; and we came home to dear mother as happy as little birds, and as fresh as the flowers, and as rosy-cheeked as the apples we carried in our hands. That was for a small moment, when we lived in happy dreamland.

He died in August, 1886, his experiences of the world prolonged many years beyond the point at which men were considered old in those times. He was 91½ years old, but his tombstone, wayward in its information as John Woodcock Graves was in his life, gives his age as 100 years.

4

The Maid of the Inn

a story drawn from our own ground
Wordsworth, The Prelude

As John Peel was setting out on the career which would win
him world fame as a hunting man, another native Cumbrian
of the opposite sex had a sort of fame thrust upon her. Peel
did not altogether dislike the public notice he won; Mary
Robinson, the Beauty of Buttermere, almost certainly hated
it when the world shone the limelight on her.

Mary, daughter of the keeper of the inn "under the sign of
the Char" at Buttermere – now the Fish Hotel – lived a
fairly normal life for a girl in her circumstances. She also
served the customers at the inn, and it was in this capacity
that she first attracted the attention of a visitor who
happened also to be a writer.

Joseph Palmer, who also wrote under the name of Joseph,
or Captain, Budworth, visited Buttermere in 1792. There he
met Mary Robinson, and in his *Fortnight's Ramble in the
Lakes*, he described his first encounter with 'The Maid of the
Inn'.

Her mother and she were spinning woollen yarn in the back kitchen.
On our going into it the girl flew away as swift as a mountain sheep,
and it was not till our return from Scale Force we could say we first
saw her.

She brought in part of our dinner, and seemed about fifteen. Her
hair was thick and long, of a dark brown, and though unadorned
with ringlets, did not seem to want them. Her face was a fine oval,
with full eyes and lips red as vermillion. Her cheeks had more of the
lily than the rose, and although she had never been out of the
village – and I hope she will never have the ambition to wish it – she
had a manner about her which seemed calculated to set off her dress
than 'dress her'; she was a very Lavinia 'seeming when unadorned,
adorned the most.'

50

Mary was baptised at Lorton Church — Buttermere was then part of the Lorton parish — on July 9, 1779, thirteen years before Palmer first saw her, but he could have been correct about her age because the children of the time often walked to their baptisms.

Whether she was thirteen or fifteen, Palmer had started the legend of the Beauty of Buttermere. On publication of his *Fortnight's Ramble* the visitors started to arrive. Wordsworth, Southey, de Quincey and Coleridge all went to see this treasure the visiting writer had unearthed at Buttermere. They seem all to have been unimpressed by her beauty, yet all gave her full marks for an excellent bearing and disposition.

Palmer's panegyric notwithstanding, Mary continued to serve the customers at the Inn, which was enjoying a trade bigger than old Joseph Robinson had ever hoped for in his wildest dreams. They found a girl, chaste and modest, who retained her native dignity despite the frankly appraising stares of visiting bucks who had made the journey to eye this equivalent of the twentieth-century sex symbol.

On a return visit, Palmer was present at a dance — the 'Merry Night' held for the benefit of the local fiddler — when he mixed freely with the company.

> They were the very rosiest cheeked mortals I ever saw. The men kept excellent time and rattled on the floor with a variety of steps; the women danced as easily as the men determinedly. The dance was never long, and the moment the fiddler ceased another set that were ready called a fresh tune and began.
>
> I was glad to notice a black-eyed youth hand out Mary and another girl and call for a reel, and I honestly say I never saw more graceful dancing or a woman of finer figure to set it off than Mary of Buttermere.

Palmer, and many others, were later to deplore that he had not left Mary to blush unseen as the Rose of Buttermere, and even before the momentous events of 1802 which were to bring poor Mary under the publiz gaze more than ever before, he seems to have had some misgivings.

Five years after the publication of his book, Palmer was back at Buttermere, apparently because of these misgivings, and proceeded to make matters worse.

He took her by the hand and said: "Mary, I wrote it, and rejoice in having had such an opportunity of minutely observing the propriety of your behaviour. You may remember I advised you in that book never to leave your native valley. Your age and situation require the utmost care. Strangers will come, and have come to see you; and some of them with very bad intentions. We hope you will never suffer from them, but never cease to be on your guard." Palmer meant well; probably felt he had some sort of responsibility for the girl's welfare, but one wonders what Mary thought of this address to her by the man who had brought her a sort of fame.

Even more interesting would be her opinion of the sting Palmer kept for the tail of his address to the Maid of the Inn. "You really are not," he said, "as handsome as you promised to be." Mary reacted admirably, for, according to Palmer, she thanked him and said: "I hope, sir, I ever have, and trust I shall always take care of myself."

Some visitors noted on her a fleeting expression of discontent; almost all found her not to be the beauty that Palmer had claimed her to be. She passed into her twenties without any sign of future wedded bliss. This was probably not for want of wooers; even for wooers with honourable intentions, but rather because Mary, her head turned by the attention lavished upon her was thinking, for matrimonial purposes 'above her station', or as it would be put locally 'abeun hersell'.

She was eventually wooed and wed by a man who probably seemed like the prince out of a fairy tale book to this girl of such humble station in the Vale of Buttermere.

'Colonel the Hon. Alexander Augustus Hope' had come to Keswick some time previously. Keswick was not wanting a celebrity or two at the time because the Lake District had become a popular resort for the titled and wealthy. But the Member of Parliament of Linlithgow and brother of the immensely rich Earl of Hopetoun, Colonel Hope made an impression on the town and people, and lived in some style at the *Royal Oak*.

He was accepted by almost everybody as the man he said

he was, and the townsfolk felt in some way flattered that such an important man should settle in their midst. He moved in the highest circles that could be found in Keswick, but a few — very few — of Keswick's residents had some reservations about Colonel Hope.

Among them was Samuel Taylor Coleridge, who had been living at Greta Hall since 1800. The Colonel's 'breeding and deportment'. aroused Coleridge's suspicion, for although the man put on a show, there was, as De Quincey was later to relate in his *Life of Coleridge*, "a tang of vulgarity about it". Coleridge also assured De Quincey that Colonel Hope was grossly ungrammatical in his ordinary conversation.

However, the Colonel went on his merry way, for although he was the object of some suspicion, he probably did not know it, and he was the lion of some of the local parties whose hostesses considered themselves lucky when he accepted their invitations.

The people accepted him because of his easy way, and when he not only received letters in his name, but franked them in the same name, it seemed to set the seal upon his genuineness. It would be argued, if the matter was discussed at all, that since forgery was a capital offence, nobody would risk a hanging solely for the sake of keeping up appearances.

Suspicion flared again when the Hon. Augustus began to pay his addresses to a young lady of beauty and good fortune who was staying at Keswick in the company of an Irish family headed by a Mr Nathaniel More. He proposed to the young lady and was accepted, and the wedding clothes were bought and the wedding date fixed. Almost as an after-thought the young lady suggested that the Colonel should also approach her friend Mr More, who was acting *in loco parentis*, about the coming nuptials. The Colonel wrote letters, and while ostensibly awaiting replies, said he would visit his cousin's seat in Scotland. Instead, he went to Buttermere and married Mary, the Beauty.

It is difficult from surviving accounts to sort out the chronology of the courtship of Colonel Hope and the Beauty of Buttermere. One report says that he was at Buttermere, staying "by the sign of the Char" for two months before the marriage, but he probably paid more than one visit. He arrived in his own carriage, but without any servants, to take part in, or to witness the char fishing, an occupation which had become something of a tourist attraction because char was a fish considered peculiar to the Lakes, and, potted, was popular as a Cumberland delicacy. At any rate he paid court to the Beauty of Buttermere, and was accepted. They were married by licence at Lorton Church, by the Minister, John Nicholson on October 2, 1802, with John Gill and Isaac Nicholson as witnesses. Both Mary and her bridegroom signed their names in almost identical copperplate writing.

To live happily ever after would in the circumstances to be related, have been impossible, but they might have enjoyed considerably more married life had it not been for Coleridge's proclivity for journalism, and the same writer's doubts about 'the Hon. Alexander Augustus Hope'.

The London morning newspaper *The Sun* carried the story of the marriage of the Beauty of Buttermere in its issue of October 11, and the article clearly underlined the doubts about the bridegroom which Coleridge, who was responsible for the article, had felt. "On the 2nd inst." the report went, "a Gentleman calling himself Alexander Augustus Hope, Member for Linlithgow, and brother to the Earl of Hopetoun, was married at the Church of Lorton, near Keswick, to a young woman, celebrated by the tourists under the name of The Beauty of Buttermere." With astounding frankness the writer went on to discuss Mary Robinson's celebrated good looks: "To beauty, however, in the strict sense of the word, she has small pretensions, for she is rather gap-toothed, and somewhat pock-fretten." Having delivered himself of that example of what could be journalistically defended as 'fair comment', he proceeded to lard the pill:

> But her face is very expressive, and the expression very interesting, and her figure and movements are graceful to a miracle. She ought to have been called The Grace of Buttermere, rather than The Beauty.
>
> She is the daughter of an old couple named Robinson, who keep a poor little pot-house at the foot of the small lake of Buttermere, with the sign of the Char, and has been all her life the attendant and waiter, for they have no servant. She is now about thirty [wrong, she was about 25], and has long attracted the notice of every visitor by her exquisite elegance and the becoming manner in which she is used to fillet her beautiful long hair; likewise by the uncommonly fine

Italian handwriting in which the little bill was drawn out.

Added to this, she has ever maintained an irreproachable character, as a good daughter, and a modest, sensible and observant woman.

That such a woman should find a husband in a man of rank and fortune so very far above her sphere of life is not extra-ordinary; but there are other circumstances which add much to the interest of the story.

Here *The Sun* pointed out that when the Colonel went to Buttermere he had announced himself — or at least the locals called him — 'The Honourable Charles Hope, Member for Dumfries'. "The mistake in his name, the want of an establishment suited to his rank . . . excited much suspicion, and many began to consider him an impostor," said *The Sun*.

However, his marriage to Mary of Buttermere had weakened suspicion, but, *The Sun* continued;

> The interest which the good people of Keswick take in the welfare of the Beauty of Buttermere has not yet suffered them entirely to subside, and they await with anxiety the moment when they shall receive decisive proofs that the bridegroom is the real person he describes himself to be.
> The circumstances of his marriage are sufficient to satisfy us that he is no imposter, and therefore we may venture to congratulate the Beauty of Buttermere upon her good fortune.

Congratulations was hardly in order.

The Sun's account of the wedding, and the suspicion which had been so freely expressed in it led to inquiries, and one of the answers received was that Colonel the Honourable Alexander Augustus Hope was abroad and had been for some time. The Beauty of Buttermere's husband, therefore, was an imposter.

The Sun of Saturday, November 6, 1802 tells the story under the headline, "The Keswick Imposter":

> A discovery has at last been made of this extra-ordinary person.
> Letters were on Thursday received in town, in answer to inquiries which had been set on foot for this paper, from which it appears that the real name of the pretended Hon. Colonel Hope is John Hatfield, a person against whom a Commission of Bankrupt was issued some months ago, to which he never surrendered; in consequence of which, in addition to other circumstances known of him, he is guilty of a capital offence, it being a felony, without

benefit of Clergy, not to surrender within the appropriate time to a Commission of Bankrupt.

About a twelvemonth ago this man had the address to introduce himself as a partner in a respectable house at Tiverton in Devonshire. In this character he visited London several times in the course of last winter; and from his specious manner and gentlemanlike demeanour, he was well received by several merchants in the city, some of whom gave him credit to a considerable amount. His drafts afterwards meeting with dishonour, an alarm was taken. Hatfield ran away from Tiverton, and a Commission issued against him, on which he was declared a bankrupt.

The effects he left behind him were inconsiderable, it being supposed that he was not backward in taking with him all the property he could collect.

A small estate in Cheshire forms the chief part of the funds wherewith his creditors are to be paid.

From the accounts which appeared in the papers of the imposter at Keswick, an idea was entertained that the elegant Colonel Hope might possibly be the same man with the specious Mr Hatfield, the manufacturer; and the assignees accordingly set on foot an inquiry the result of which is, that in opening some boxes which were left behind at Keswick, several letters were found directed to him by his proper name of Hatfield.

He has a wife and family now living at Tiverton; so that in marrying the unfortunate Mary of Buttermere, he has added bigamy to his list of offences.

Realising that his game was up, Hatfield fled from Buttermere. His escape was made the easier because it was obvious that some of the people around Keswick still had sufficient faith in him to lend him money — in the name he had assumed.

He went down the coast to Ravenglass where he found refuge on a ship for a few days before heading for Chester and later into Wales where he was arrested near Swansea by the Bow Street Runners who were on his trail.

After his arrest, Hatfield was taken to London for examination by the magistrates where charges of forgery were brought against him. A letter which he had signed in his assumed name was produced as evidence. The secondary charge was bigamy and as evidence of this a letter was produced from his wife still living at Tiverton, and a certificate of his marriage to the Beauty of Buttermere.

He was committed to Carlisle Assizes for trial. He was found guilty on three charges of forgery after a trial in the

Town Hall which had lasted eight hours. He was sentenced to death, and thought it was not expected that he would hang for his crime, there was no reprieve and he was hanged on The Sands between the two Eden bridges at Carlisle on September 3, 1803.

Wordsworth and Coleridge were passing through Carlisle while Hatfield was under sentence of death, and they sought an interview with him. Wordsworth was admitted, but Hatfield refused to see Coleridge, whom he had carefully avoided during his stay at Keswick. This early avoidance of Coleridge was now being attributed to the fact that the poet, like Hatfield, had connections in Devon, and he was afraid he might be recognised. His refusal to see Coleridge in Carlisle gaol was probably because he regarded the writer as the architect of his downfall through the article which had appeared in the London newspapers.

Before the Hatfield affair, Mary, the Beauty of Buttermere had been a tourist attraction on whom visitors had felt themselves permitted to pass opinions as they might on the view from Ashness Bridge or Castle Head. After it, she was raised to the status of a national figure.

She had figured little in the evidence which was offered against Hatfield, her only contribution being a note in her impeccable copperplate hand to the London examining magistrate which stated:

> The man whom I had the misfortune to marry, and who has ruined me and my parents, always told me he was the Hon. Colonel Hope, the next brother of the Earl of Hopetoun.
>   Your grateful and obedient servant,
>   Mary Robinson.

Hatfield's bigamous marriage with Mary was, in the eyes of the law, a lesser crime than forgery, and it was for the forgery that he was sentenced to die. But, it was said at the time, there might have been a reprieve for him had he not deceived Mary of Buttermere.

It was this association that caught the imagination of the public. As de Quincey writes in his *Life of Coleridge*:

> Dramas and melo-dramas were produced in the London Theatres upon her story; and for many years afterwards shoals of tourists

crowded to the secluded lake, and the little homely cabaret, which had been the scene of her brief romance.

"It was fortunate for a person in her distressing situation that her home was not in a town . . . the few and simple neighbours . . . treated it as an unmixed injury reflecting shame on nobody but the wicked perpetrator.

"Hence, without much trial to her womanly sensibilities, she found herself able to resume her situation at the little inn; and this she continued to hold for many years.

The Lake poets all, according to de Quincey, admired Mary greatly, always, however, with some reservations about her entitlement to Palmer's original description. De Quincey wrote:

Her figure was, in my eyes good; but I doubt whether most of my readers would have thought it such. She was none of your evanescent, wasp-waisted beauties; on the contrary, she was rather large in every way, tallish and proportionately broad. Her face was fair and her features feminine; and unquestionably she was what all the world would have agreed to call 'good looking'.

Beautiful in an emphatic sense she was not. Everything about her face and bust was negative; simply without offence. Even this, however, was more than could be said at all times, for the expression of her countenance was often disagreeable. This arose out of her situation; connected as it was with defective sensibility, and a misdirected pride.

De Quincey appreciated the situation in which Mary of Buttermere found herself and made some allowance for her reaction to the spotlight which had been turned on her and made her into something which was part tourist attraction and part freak.

Men who had no touch of a gentleman's nature in their composition, sometimes insulted her by looks and by words: and she too readily attributed the same spirit of impertinent curiosity to every man whose eyes happened to settle upon her face.

Yet once at least I must have seen her under the most favourable circumstances: for on my first visit to Buttermere, I had the pleasure of Mr Southey's company, who was incapable of wounding anybody's feelings, and to Mary, in particular, was well known by kind attentions, and I believe by some services. Then at least I saw her to advantage, and perhaps for a figure of her build, at the best age, for it was about nine or ten years after her misfortune, when she might be twenty-seven or twenty-eight years old. [Mary had worn better than de Quincey knew, for his estimate of her 'best' age was seven or eight years short of her actual age at the time.]

We were alone, a solitary pair of tourists: nothing arose to confuse or distress her. She waited upon us at dinner, and talked to us freely. 'This is a respectable young woman,' I said to myself.

Of course, Wordsworth came into the picture. Like others, he had been over to Buttermere to inspect the beauty Palmer had discovered, and though nothing is reported of what he said or thought at the time, he did save his opinions until after the Hatfield incident.

In *The Prelude*, which he finished in 1805, he gave mention of Mary in what he called "a story drawn from our own ground", and after briefly touching upon the Hatfield affair, went on to recall

> the moment when we first,
> Ere the broad world rang with the maiden's name,
> Beheld her serving at the cottage inn;
> Both stricken, as she entered and withdrew
> With admiration of her modest mien
> And carriage, marked by unexampled grace.

Wordsworth continues to speak of Mary:

> Unspoiled by commendation and the excess
> Of public — notice and offensive light
> To a meek spirit suffering inwardly.

And then, after Hatfield:

> She lives in peace
> Upon the spot where she was born and reared;
> Without contamination doth she live
> In quietness, without anxiety:
> Beside the mountain chapel, sleeps in earth
> Her new-born infant.

Later in the same work, Wordsworth again mentions

> Thy nameless babe that sleeps
> Beside the mountain chapel undisturbed.

Wordsworth's mention of the "nameless babe" suggests that the child which Mary bore to Hatfield was either stillborn or died in infancy; at any rate there is no record of the baptism of the child in the Lorton Parish Register.

Usually quite accurate in his topography, Wordsworth is wrong in giving the Buttermere chapel a graveyard. Scornfully, Frederick Reed of Hassness, told F.E. Edwards in 1874: "There is not and never had been a burial ground at Buttermere, and it would puzzle folk to make graves in the rock on which the present chapel stands and the late chapel stood." Mary's unnamed infant was probably buried at Lorton.

Even de Quincey, long after the event and all that had been written about it, was hazy about the Buttermere chapel, so perhaps Wordsworth can be excused. De Quincey obviously knew the chapel well because he wrote a touchingly beautiful piece about it in his reference to Mary of Buttermere.

I do not know whether the marriage was, or could have been celebrated in the little mountain chapel of Buttermere. [He obviously didn't take the trouble to find out, which is just as well or he might not have continued]. I persuade myself that the most hardened villain must have felt a momentary pang on violating the altar of such a chapel, so touchingly does it express, by its miniature dimensions, the almost helpless humility of that little pastoral community to whose spiritual wants it has from generation to generation administered. It is not only the smallest chapel by many degrees in all England, but it is so mere a toy in outwards appearance that, were it not for its antiquity, its wild mountain exposure, and its consecrated connection with the final hopes and fears of the adjacent pastoral hamlet — but for these considerations, the first movement of a stranger's feelings would be towards loud laughter, for the little chapel looks not so much a mimic chapel in a drop scene from the Opera House, as a miniature copy from such a scene; and evidently could not receive within its walls more than half a dozen households.

Buttermere Church was not licensed for marriages until about 1864.

Mary continued to work at the inn for about ten years after Hatfield, a ten-year stint, no doubt, if she was as human as she seems to have been, of fighting back her desires, the principal one of which must have been to smash her next tray of food or drinks upon the heads of the goggling visitors.

Eventually there came another man into her life. Richard Harrison, son of Richard Harrison, of Todcrofts, Caldbeck, came to Buttermere, probably on business to do with Herdwick sheep, since the farmers of Caldbeck and the farmers of Buttermere all kept the same breed.

He saw, met and married Mary of Buttermere when she was over 30 years old. The match was a happy one. Mary's parents had aged, and she and Dick Harrison kept the Buttermere inn for some time before he inherited Todcrofts at Ireby, and they moved to Caldbeck.

Mary died on February 7, 1837, at the age of fifty-eight, and lies under the imposing gravestone in Caldbeck churchyard. Her ultimate triumph was her later life in that she was able to lead it as a normal, respectable farm wife, and bring up a family. To outward appearance, at any rate, she remained unspoiled by her tragedy.

Perhaps the not over-perspicacious Wordsworth found in the Mary he knew some inward hurt, for in *The Prelude* he wrote that he had observed:

> Her just opinions, delicate reserve,
> Her patience and humility of mind
> Unspoiled by commendation and the excess
> Of public notice — an offensive light
> To a meek spirit suffering inwardly.

5

Valley of the Black Diamonds

Bentley Beetham busily gardening on crags with his trowel; an early morning start to climb Black Crag Buttress in Troutdale; a 'geography walk' from school to see the great ice-scored boiler-plates of slate near Bowder Stone; innumerable visits to Seathwaite, allegedly the wettest place in Britain, without ever having been there in rain; the rock-strewn chaotic aftermath of the great cloudburst of August 13, 1966 . . . these are memories of Borrowdale. These, and months of Sundays climbing and walking from Seathwaite, up the Sty to Gable and Scawfell, up Langstrath where the lure of bathing in spectacular pools was stronger than the urge to continue walking; scratching the waste heaps of the graphite mine looking for scraps of the elusive wadd; shaking hands with a friend under Bowder Stone and wishing a wish.

To anybody from the western side of Cumberland, Borrowdale is the Lake District, or the heart of it. It has been the bone of many a contention, threatened with despoilation, rescued and threatened again, and it has had more 'lives' in the struggle between would-be despoilers and the amenities societies than any other part of the Lake Country, and has yet managed to remain unspoiled.

With his trowel, cleaning sods and clods from niches in the crags to expose sound rock and pioneer new climbing routes up hitherto unconsidered rocks, Bentley Beetham opened up Borrowdale to an invasion by young men in knee breeches, 'Vibrum' boots and red stockings who hang decoratively, and dangerously by fingerholds and from red ropes on Shepherd's and other Borrowdale crags.

Man's occupation of Borrowdale has a long history. The top of an old quern found in Troutdale, and ancient fortifications on Castle Crag and on Reecastle beside Lodore indicate how long.

Prehistoric man's apparent preoccupation with defence, and the secretive manner of his successors indicate that Borrowdale was either a locality of great value, or a place of refuge from the several waves of invaders of the Cumbrian countryside: a secret place. And since the land of the dale has never been excessively kind to the men who have worked it, saving a few fortunes made out of its famous 'wadd', the value of the place seems to have been in its isolation.

It was its inaccessibility which gave Borrowdale a special significance, its people a special character — not entirely good — and the whole — fells, crags, forests, streams and people — a sort of mysterious quality which drew out the best, and worst, of the early 'Lakers.'

There was a grimness about The Jaws which deterred early writers, and one of these was Thomas Gray who stopped at Grange and refused to go any further. This was fortunate because it was at Grange that Gray wrote one of the choicer passages in his immortal *Journal*. "The crags named Lodore Banks" he wrote, "begin now to impend terribly over the way, and more terribly when you hear that three years since [he was writing in 1796] an immense mass of rock tumbled at once from the brow, barring all access to the dale (for this was the only road) till they could work their way through it." At Gowdar Crag he was warned to pass in silence lest the reverberation of voices should bring down the impending rocks.

Gray went on to say that the path onwards up the valley was so difficult that "all further access is here barred to prying mortals, only there is a little path winding over the fells, and for some weeks of the year passable to the dalesmen, but the mountains know well that these innocent people will not reveal the mysteries of their ancient kingdom 'the reign of Chaos and Old Night.' "

It is likely that Gray was having his leg pulled, that he had encountered some early Borrowdale 'gowks' who were even then building up the Borrowdale legend. Auld Will Ritson was not the pioneer tall story teller in the Lake District. Or maybe Gray met up with the advance guard of Borrowdale's strictly unofficial security forces which protected the goings-on up the valley from prying eyes. From their obviously untrue reference to the little path over the fells "passable only for some weeks of the year" they were indeed hiding the mysteries of their ancient kingdom, like the smugglers' route over Sty Head by which the rum came in and the illicit wadd went out.

An earlier writer than Gray had encountered some of the diggers for illicit wadd, and his account of the incident reads something like that of an explorer in Darkest Africa coming across a tribe hitherto unseen by civilised man.

'G.S.' (probably George Smith of Wigton, who was a regular contributor to the *Gentleman's Magazine*, mostly on the antiquities of Cumberland) set out from Wigton in 1749 to explore Borrowdale.[1] Near the head of the valley, he wrote, "We had not ascended very far before we perceived some persons at a very great distance above us who seemed to be very busy though we could not distinguish what they were doing. As soon as they saw us, they hastily left their work, and were running away, but by a signal made by our guide, who probably was but too well acquainted with them they returned, to the number of eighteen."

But it was not the shyness of the noble savage that caused these fellside workers to scuttle; they were digging with mattocks and other instruments in a heap of clay and rubbish near the older wadd mines. These old spoil heaps, neglected by the mine-owners as affording nothing worth the search, could provide wadd enough for these illicit diggers to clear six or eight shillings a day. Digging for illicit wadd seems to have been a worth-while occupation: worth the attendant risks since it was against the law to dig for it, even on the waste heaps.

The bold 'G.S.', in whose footsteps Gray later feared to tread, carried on with his exploration to "the summit of the black-lead hill" where "we were astonished to perceive a large plain to the west, and from thence another craggy ascent of five hundred yards, as near as I could guess. The whole mountain is called 'Unnesterre' or, as I suppose "Finisterre'." He was of course writing about Honister.

He strode on to the summit and found: "The scene was

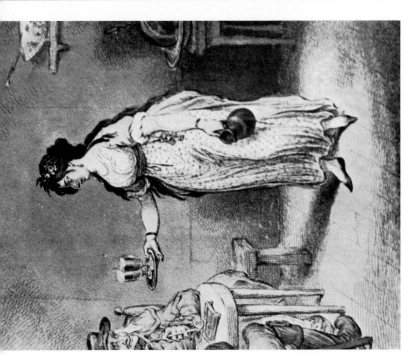

Mary of Buttermere: (left) 'sketched from life' in July 1800 before she married Hatfield, and published November 1802, after her unfortunate marriage had hit the headlines; (right) sketched, according to the inscription, in 1806 by Lieut.-Col. Wylliams

Buttermere Church and village. The most distant building is the
Fish Inn, once home of Mary, the Beauty of Buttermere

terrifying; not an herb to be seen, but wild savine growing in the interstices of the naked rocks; the horrid projection of vast promontories, the vicinity of the clouds, the thunder of the explosions in the slate quarries, the dreadful solitude, the distance of the plain below, and the mountains heaped on mountains that were piled around us, desolate and waste, like the ruins of a world we have survived, excited such ideas of horror as are not to be expressed."

If 'G.S.' was disturbed by the thunder of explosions in the slate quarries on Honister it is evidence that at least one aspect of the advancing technology of the time had reached this primitive outpost of England.

Obviously Borrowdale presented a challenge to the explorers of the time because, in terms of other attainable or unattainable objects of later years 'it was there', and 'G.S.' chalked up a gleeful 'first', noting that in the previous year the expedition had been attempted by a certain "ingenious Mr Bower" — "but he got no higher than the chapel".

It is an interesting thought for modern visitors to Borrowdale that the little church at Stonethwaite should mark the limit of Mr Bower's penetration of the dale, a sort of Camp Six in this Everest among valleys.

Before a road was built into Borrowdale to take anything wider than a packhorse, the Borrowdale folk communicated with the outside world only as much as they had to. They dealt at Keswick market, but there was probably as much contact with the Buttermere, Wasdale and Wythburn valleys because these equally remote places had more in common with Borrowdale than rumbustious Keswick which, at its worst during the height of the copper-mining era, probably had something of the atmosphere of a mining town in California or the Klondyke.

The Borrowdalians needed little communication with Keswick because they were mainly self-sufficient. Their sheep provided them with food and clothing, with plenty to spare of both for barter for things they could not grow or rear. The Derwent gave them fish — but, strangely enough, no salmon — and the thin soil of their fields grew grain enough to see them through the winter. The valley was also self-sufficient in salt, at once both a necessity and a luxury, which was produced from the salt spring at Brandlehow.

For almost half the year the head of the valley could be cut off by floods or snow which rendered the paths impassable. When they could get down to Keswick, the dalesfolk went on horseback with a sod of turf or a bundle of hay for a saddle, and if the horse ate the saddle whilst in Keswick the ride home was less painful than it would have been if the ale in Keswick had been less strong.

In his *Survey of the Lakes*, in 1787, James Clarke, of Kendal, wrote:

> Borrowdale till within these last thirty years was hardly in a state even of civilisation; the surface of the ground was very little cultivated, for agriculture was not understood there, and the inhabitants were a proverb even among their unpolished neighbours, for ignorance.
>
> Not above twenty years ago a cart, or any kind of wheel carriage, was totally unknown in Borrowdale; in carrying home their hay (for they make no stacks) they lay it upon their horses in bundles, one on each side; yet, strange to tell, so bigoted are the inhabitants, even in the more civilised parts, that they obstinately adhere to this absurd custom . . . Their food in summer consisted of fish and small mutton; in winter they lived upon bacon and hung mutton. Nor was their manner of drying their mutton less rude; they hung their sheep up by the hinder legs, and took away nothing but the head and entrails. In this situation I have seen seven sheep hanging in one chimney, and have been told of much greater numbers.

Smoked mutton was revived at the start of the second World War as a substitute for bacon, of which a shortage was forecast. In a fit of inspiration somebody called it 'macon', but it never caught on, even in Borrowdale.

As Borrowdale became more civilised, and, no doubt, after early visitors had found it difficult to stomach meat cut from whole carcases hanging in chimneys, the practice of smoking mutton for winter food ceased, and bacon took over.

Still the huge chimneys with which almost all Borrowdale's old stone houses were furnished came in useful, and so great was their capacity that smoking other people's bacon became another branch of Borrowdale's cottage industry. At the start of winter, 1882 the great chimney of Caffle House in Watendlath had in it, apart from the family's own stock, over thirty hams and flitches of bacon smoking for Parson Battersby, of Keswick.

Winter was the enemy in Borrowdale, against whom the

dalesfolk prepared all their defences. "Winter's allus coming," said one old dalesman, by which he meant that the efforts of the people for most of the year were spent in getting ready for it.

They were provident people; they had to be to survive, and it was perhaps their preoccupation with winter which led to the "auld wife santer" about the Borrowdalians trying to wall in the cuckoo to ensure eternal spring.

The wall, they still say, was built one course too low, and the cuckoo escaped; escaped from the valley but not from its lore, and Borrowdalians are still called — and like to be called — 'gowks', which is the dialect name for cuckoos. That it is also the dialect name for fools is, to the Borrowdalians, a matter of no importance.

The Borrowdalians' ready acceptance of the 'gowk' tag was due to the fact that they themselves thought highly of the bird, and Jobby Wilson, a scion of the Wilsons of Watendlath, and a writer of good, sensible, homely dialect, said that gowks came in many forms in Borrowdale. There were the apple gowks (apple fools) which the children liked; April gowks, reserved for revelation on the first of April; gowks who thought they were clever, and gowks who knew they were fools.

Then, of course, the bird gowks were not gowks at all since they found a lot of pleasure and very little hard work in their world. "If," said Jobby Wilson, "there were more gowks there would be better crops in the fields and more fruit in the gardens, because the cuckoo is as fond of hairyworms and caterpillars as the blackbird is of gooseberries."

Writing to the *West Cumberland Times* in 1885 after he had emigrated to New England, Jobby's thoughts on the cuckoo were put this way: "Fwoak may think 'at t' cuckoo charms t' weather, an' fetches t' Spring on its grey wings, shouten' aw t' woods an' meadas to waken up as Spring's cumt, bit if they'd kept their eyes an' ears oppen they wad ha' nwoatish'd 'at t' Spring's here day an' days afoor t' cuckoo's astir."

The cuckoo as the harbinger of spring notwithstanding, the weather had other agents controlling it, for the ancient folklore of the dale (again as related by Jobby Wilson) tells of twelve silent men, every one of them holding a 'pore' (poker) sitting around a fire which never goes out. Three of them have cloaks as green as grass; three gold as ripe corn; three blood-red as wine, and three as white as snow. These twelve men are the months of the year, and the fire which never goes out is the sun. Every man 'rowkes' (pokes) the fire in turn, but if one of them happens to sleep over, as sometimes they will, then the next one takes his turn, and the consequence is that the seasons go wrong, and there is frost and snow where there should be sunshine and showers, or sunshine and showers where there should be frost and snow.

The legend of the cuckoo wall led to other fables, like the one about the red deer stag which escaped over the fells from Armboth, and so cleverly eluded all the dalesfolk's attempts to catch it, that they became convinced that it was a witch.

From the ridiculous to the outrageous went the follies of the gowks. The first mule in the valley, so one tale goes, aroused considerable interest. It was neither horse nor ass: everybody knew that. The valley's wise man was called in, and he ran through an obviously limited list of the things he had seen and which this strange new animal could not be, and came at last to something he had heard about and had never seen, and decided that the animal must be a peacock!

More believable is the story of the dalesman who brought the first load of quick lime into the upper reaches of the valley, an inspired purchase on the part of some tiller of this extremely acid soil. He was coming through The Jaws by the river path when it started to rain. As the rain penetrated the sacks the lime started to emit clouds of steam. The carrier thought this was a fire and threw water from the Derwent on it, which made things much worse before, in a panic, he unhitched the loads from the packhorses and dumped them in the river.

The dalesmen's penchant for telling tall stories, and the wealth of lore they built around themselves came, no doubt, from their Norse ancestors, and like the Norsemen they believed in witchcraft and the special qualities of the rowan tree, the sacred ash.

They used the need-fire to cure or ward off cattle diseases, and kept a rowan stick in the dairy to ensure that cream would churn quickly into butter; gave a new-born calf a handful of salt to ensure that it lived and became fruitful, and put some salt on a sod on the breast of a corpse.[2]

As they were reluctant to introduce wheeled vehicles, a reluctance which is easily explained since there were no roads suitable for such vehicles, so too were they reluctant to put aside old customs, like counting their sheep the 'old' way — yan, tyan, tethera, methera, pimp; sethera, lethera, hovera, dovera, dick, and so on. How old? As old as counting itself, since the yan, pimp and dick are first cousins to the one, five and ten of most of the languages of the world.

From time to time it is said that the old sheep-counting method is still in use. It is not, but it is unlikely to be lost or forgotten — not as long as anybody is interested in the Lake Country; not as long as there is anybody to come and look, read and listen, and say any of the variations on "Isn't it cute!"

Counting sheep has long been recommended as a soporific, but with most insomniacs it does not work because the imagination is working too hard at conjuring up a picture of sheep 'lowping' a dyke or passing through a 'hogg whoal'. Yan, tyan, tethera, methera, pimp; sethera, lethera, hovera, dovera, dick . . . insomniacs should try counting their sheep, or just counting, slowly to themselves in the old way; it has a rhythm with it of repetitive, soft consonants, like the sound of bees crowding the flowers of an old sycamore on a lazy summer afternoon: the perfect lullaby.

After the Norman Conquest, William's influence did not reach the Lake District in time for any part of it to be mentioned in the Domesday Book. Cumbria was then part of Scotland. Rufus appropriated it to the English crown, and when the Norman barons of Allerdale, of which the Western Lakes became part, realised what they had gained: a poor and unproductive district wrought by descendants of the original Norse settlers who were distant, proud and anything but co-operative with the new masters, they were not over anxious in exploiting their property.

It was the monks of Furness who first realised the advantages of Borrowdale as a sheep run, and the Coucher Book of Furness shows that in 1209 the monks of that great Cistercian house bought, at a total cost of £156 13s 4d, the lands of Borrowdale, from Alice de Romelli, daughter of William fitz Duncan, who, owing to the death of her brother William, the 'Boy of Egremont', in the waters of the Strid in Yorkshire, had inherited the barony of Allerdale.

During the Dissolution of the Monasteries, Borrowdale went to Henry VIII, and two of the dalesmen, John Fyssher and his son Lancelot were appointed bailiffs, answering for rents amounting to £24 14s.

The names on the rent rolls are interesting because most of them remain, if not in the valley and on their original tenements, at least in the district: John Hynde, Robert Udale, Nicholas Fisher, Thomas Fysher, Myles Birkhead, John Birkhead (the original of the modern name Birkett, also spelt Byrkhed, Burkehead and Birkehead), Hugh Richardson, John Braithwaite, Thomas Dyconson, John Jobson. Phonetically, this is a roll call of almost any gathering of deep-rooted dalesmen of today.

The same families lived for upwards of four centuries on the same tenements in Borrowdale, and most of them could still be found on the land of their ancestors in the middle of the nineteenth century.

By 1615 the farmers of Borrowdale were able to buy their land, the land they and their ancestors had worked for centuries. James I who was selling some of the Crown lands granted Borrowdale to William Whitmore and James Verdon, of London, a pair of Stuart-time property speculators, and they sold it in thirty-seven lots. Under the Great Deed of Borrowdale, which concerns that piece of property dealing, the tenants purchased their lands and all mineral and manorial rights, "except all those wad holes, commonly called Black Cawke, within the commons of Seatoller."

Whitmore and Verdon later sold the wadd mines to John Lamplugh and Charles Hudson for £25 2s, and in 1622 Lamplugh sold his share to John Bankes, of Keswick, father of Sir John Bankes, benefactor to his native town, and after coming into the possession of the Bankes family, the mines were "wrought with great success".

When fortunes began to be made out of graphite it, no doubt, surprised the people of Borrowdale who had known of its existence for some time, and had used it for marking

their sheep. That they indulged in the illicit trade for wadd is
certain; and there is the evidence of 'G.S.' who saw the
diggers at work on the waste heaps during his exploration of
the dale. Knowledge of the country and native cunning
enabled them not only to collect the wadd, but to get it out
of the district by secret routes to the *Bunch of Grapes* (now
the George Hotel) at Keswick, which was a meeting place for
those engaged in trading with illicit wadd, and to other
outlets at the ports on the Cumberland coast.

But for a quirk of Nature, the graphite mines of
Borrowdale could have been a counterpart of the great
diamond 'pipes' of South Africa. So said John Postlethwaite,
whose *Mines and Mining in the Lake District* is the best and
most comprehensive work on the subject.

Postlethwaite was coldly accurate in his writing, but
occasionally strayed from the strictly scientific in his lectures
to fly a few geological kites which brought his talks to life,
and stirred up interest among his audiences in the literary and
scientific societies which sprang up in and on the fringes of
the Lake District in the late nineteenth century.

In a lecture at Keswick in March, 1914, he said, rather
sadly it seemed at the time, that under slightly changed
geological circumstances the great 'pipes' of wadd could have
been world-famous diamond mines because the chemical
make-up of diamond and wadd had very few differences, and
his theory was that the wadd had come into being in much
the same way as had the diamonds of Kimberley. Like
diamonds, said Postlethwaite, the wadd was found in sops or
pipes, mostly vertical, or nearly so, and varied in depth from
a few feet to sixty fathoms. A single pipe, discovered in 1778
yielded graphite worth £43,785 at 30s a pound, and the most
valuable strike, made in 1803, yielded graphite worth
£105,000.

There were other graphite deposits in other parts of the
world, though none of such pure mineral as the Seathwaite
wadd.

Postlethwaite argued that the graphite deposits in the
Americas originated in the same way as coal, through a
natural process of transmutation of vegetable matter into
peat; peat into lignite into coal; coal into anthracite, and

anthracite into graphite. But he could not, he said, account similarly for the presence of these huge pipes of graphite in Borrowdale, concentrated as they were in a comparatively minute area only a third of a mile long.

A few years earlier Postlethwaite had met a mining engineer who was also a mineralogist, and who also had a theory about the origin of the Borrowdale wadd. This was that the graphite was originally Plutonic soot — literally soot from the underworld — which, during Borrowdale's volcanic era had been forced up from below with molten rock, and been solidified by great heat and pressure. "There must," said Postlethwaite drily, commenting on this theory, "have been a very extensive sweeping of the Plutonic flues and chimneys in order to collect the sixty tons and more of graphite that were obtained from a few of the principal sops or pipes."

Postlethwaite would have none of this mineralogist's theory. He felt that the formation of the graphite pipes was due to roughly similar circumstances as resulted in the formation of the diamond pipes of South Africa, which were also vertical, although diving much deeper into the earth's crust. The conditions under which the Borrowdale pipes were formed, said Postlethwaite, probably approached closely to the conditions under which the diamonds of Kimberley were produced.

> We can only suppose that the molten magma, in its upwards course, passed through a mass of highly bituminous or carbonaceous material, and that it tore off and bore along with it numerous fragments large and small until it came to rest and solidified, the bituminous matter being acted upon by the heat during the process to turn it into graphite.
>
> It is interesting to know that under slightly altered conditions diamonds might have been produced instead of graphite.

Very interesting indeed! It requires no great stretch of imagination to picture Borrowdale after a diamond rush. The spoil heaps left by the old graphite-mining activities seem like the soil kicked out of holes by rabbits in comparison with the industrial scars left by larger mining operations. There might have been holes in Borrowdale to rival the great deep of Kimberley; the fells could have been torn apart in search of greater riches than ever graphite afforded; this part of the Lake Country could have been ravaged as no area of Britain has been.

The wadd mining era in Borrowdale was one of the more colourful episodes in the history of the Lake Country; it lasted a long time, but the damage was not irreparable. With Postlethwaite as their guide, aided today by a fast-growing bibliography of the geology of the Lake Country, geologists still come to Borrowdale as to the Promised Land. Here young geologists, alone and in school parties, cut their teeth in searching the left-overs of bygone mining operations, which is why some of the little waste-heaps outside the adits on the fellsides look as if they have been through a mincer.

The Borrowdale mine waste heaps have little of interest left in them. The original miners sorted their minerals carefully from the rock; Borrowdale's eighteenth-century 'pirate' miners sifted it once again, and close on a century of small-tooth-combing by amateur geologists tap-tapping with their little hammers has left practically nothing of any value, intrinsically or geologically. But still they come and search, and the chacking of their hammers through the balmy air of a warm summer afternoon sounds like wheatears' alarm calls as they stand guard on their scree strongholds.

6

Merry Nights and Taffy Joins

The catalogue of pleasures in which the inhabitants of the Lake District traditionally indulged is a long one. There were merry nights and furth nights; weddings and Christmas parties which wended their way through a valley until Twelfth Night. There were taffy joins and rum butter laitins, and the communal fun which followed boon ploughings and clay daubins; sheep shearing and corn reaping; peat cutting and hay-timing – and funerals. Sometimes the fun was of spontaneous growth; much of it was thoroughly organised to the last bite of cheese and the last sup of ale.

Whether it was a birth, a marriage or a death, a party had to have some occurrence to spark it off, and if births and marriages were truly occasions for celebration, the funeral was also a time for ensuring that the deceased was buried with what his neighbours considered honour, and remembered with a warmth which could often only be generated by frequent application to the ale barrel or the rum jar.

The garnering of the harvest was celebrated only when all had been safely gathered in, and, because of the vagaries of the Lake Country weather, this was a moveable feast. It is only in comparatively recent years that harvest festivals at churches and chapels have been fixed months ahead, usually for a time when the visitors are still there to swell the congregations and collections.

The merry night, or 'murry neet' was the occasion on which the local fiddler repaid the hospitality of the dalesmen at the end of the Christmas round of parties.

Christmas started on Christmas Eve, and for twelve days no work was done at all except for the necessary tasks of watering and feeding the stock. Every house in a valley would

74

have a party of some sort, and there was no question of who was going to which party; everybody went to every party.

Adults found their entertainment in dancing and playing cards, and demolishing seemingly unlimited piles of food and ale. The dances were fast and furious, and the card-playing was in deadly earnest. Sometimes the carding went on for two or three days in one house, after which the players would move on to catch up the party.

Most important were the fiddler and the fiddler's man, the latter acting the role of Master of Ceremonies, calling the dances and the tunes and according musical honours of everybody in the household. As Christmas wore on, the fiddler's tunes became less recognisable, and his and his man's tracks through the snow more erratic, and many a fiddler and his man could not stand the pace and spent some time sleeping it off in strange beds.

Geuse (goose) pies and 'stannin pies' were cooked in special ovens, and if a pie made of goose sounds like rich food it was poor in comparison with the 'stannin pie' which is still made in the Lake District.

The stannin pie was, as its name suggests, a 'standing' or 'raised' pie, being built into a raised crust made of warm dripping, milk and flour. On the bottom of the pie was a layer of lean mutton, cut up fine. Then the pie was filled almost to the top with currants, raisins, peel, cinnamon and brown sugar. This was topped off with shredded suet from sheep's kidneys, and another handful of raisins, and to give it that extra touch of flavour half a bottle of rum was poured into it. The pie was then baked for two hours, and the juice from the fruit and the fat, together with the rum and brown sugar, stewed the mutton. Not unnaturally, Stanning pie has a flavour all its own.

'Furth nights' were when the dalesmen's families went forth into each house of the community in turn to spend the evening around a peat fire, talking and knitting. And in some districts, especially the dales within reach of Kendal, everybody knitted: women, men, boys and girls. They talked about the weather, the state of the crops, the price of butter and the prices the Kendal merchants were offering for knitted goods; and they swopped local gossip, all the time the wooden needles rattling like some muted machinery. Perhaps there would be a reading, of a newspaper or a pamphlet, or, if the local parson happened along, of something from the Bible. The knitters used knitting sticks so that they could knit one-handed, using the spare hand to rock a cradle, fill a pipe, turn a peat, cut a slice of bread or cheese, or lift a tankard of ale.

The glow of the peat fire, flickering rushlights; the rattle of swift needles, and the rumble of a broad dialect voice telling a story or relating some gossip presents an atractive scene if it had not at the end of it the thought of Kendal merchants coming in to haggle over the price of stockings or gloves.

In areas where the knitting was not on such a commercial basis, the work done on furth nights covered a wider range, like weaving baskets, carding wool, making brooms and caulkering clogs with maybe a handloom clattering in a corner.

But a furth night was a sober occasion a get together for the dual, and rewarding objects of exchanging views and saving fuel, and the food provided was the everyday stuff, such as haver bread and potatoes, or a bit of cheese or boiled fish washed down with skim milk, tea or treacle beer.

A wedding really was a cause for celebration and an occasion of vital importance to the young people most closely concerned because the scale of the wedding often dictated the subsequent life style of the participants.

After the question had been popped, and they had been 'thrown ower t' beuks' — or had the banns called — the bride and groom-to-be toured the community 'bidding' neighbours and relatives to the wedding by word of mouth and often giving relatives the pleasure of meeting their cousin's 'intended' for the first time.

Everybody turned up at church for the wedding, mostly on horseback, and after the knot had been tied there was a rush to mount horses and race to the bride's home, often with a bridle as prize for the first arrival.

After the bride and groom had encountered such obstacles as ropes held across the road by strong young men, and through which the horses had to force their way, often leaving a few bruises in their wake, they arrived either at their

own future home, or the bride's father's house. There the
bride received the guests, seated on a stool, or 'coppy', with a
pewter dish in her lap into which every guest was expected to
put a cash contribution. One wedding at Low Lorton raised
twenty-four pounds for the young couple in this way, which
was a considerable sum of money at the time.

And then the fun began. The biggest barn in the village
would be cleared and the fiddler would put horsehair to
catgut to play for dancing while the womenfolk doled out
huge portions of cold beef, home-brewed ale and girdle cakes.

When it grew late, and it was time for the bride to be
bedded, the girls, her friends, took her to the bedroom and
tucked her in. Just before they left it was the custom for the
bride to take the stocking off her left leg and fling it over her
shoulder. Whoever caught it would be the next to wed.

An 'infair' was a sort of follow-up to a wedding because it
was a party called by a newly-wed couple, but the meaning
was lost when the infair went commercial and owners of inns
staged them purely for profit. One who cashed in on this was
old John Askew who kept the *Golden Lion* in Kirkgate,
Cockermouth, and his infairs became locally famous.

And so did the infairs and 'murry neets' at the *Pack Horse*
at Lorton. So much so that in that village the murry neet
stopped being purely seasonal and became a year-round form
of entertainment in which anybody could join on payment of
what they could afford, as long as it was between a shilling
and half a crown. Sally Chambers, hostess at the *Pack Horse*
set these limits having calculated that anything over a shilling
a head was profit, but her motives were never questioned
because she made the best 'pow-sowdy' in the district.

Pow-sowdy was a famous concoction. It was made in the
wash-house set-pot. A dozen gallons of strong ale were
warmed in the set-pot and when it was hot a quart of rum was
added, along with some cinnamon and nutmeg, and when it
was ready, rounds of crisp-toasted brown bread were cut up
and dropped in.

The pow-sowdy was dished out in basins, and it was
supped with a spoon. Connoisseurs said that it was the
warmth of the liquor and the slowness with which it was
drunk that made it so potent. And its potency was proved,

time and again, by old Dancy Dickinson, the Packhorse
fiddler, who over the years, by constant practice, had
developed a resistance to the effects of alcohol that could see
him through any round of Christmas parties and not turn a
hair until he had a basinful of Sally Chambers' pow-sowdy.
Then, and not until then, he usually passed out.

The origin of rum butter as part of the celebrations of the
birth of a child is unknown, but until recently no confinement was considered complete until the rum butter
bowl — usually a family heirloom — had been filled with this
concoction of butter, soft brown sugar, rum and nutmeg.
Rum butter is still served in parts of Cumberland to friends
and relatives who call to congratulate mothers on their
recently-delivered offspring, but like many other things, rum
butter has been commercialized, and is now sold in cardboard
tubs to visitors, and sent around the country like Devonshire
clotted cream and Yarmouth kippers and has 'Greetings from
the Lake District' printed on it.

The mystique has been taken out of rum butter. Its recipe
was never a closely-guarded secret, but it was usually made
by the elderly women of the community, most often by the
maternal grandmother of the expected child.

There is a story of an off-comer in a village who wanted to
know how to make this delicacy, and was told by one of the
female village elders: "Time enough for thee ta know hoo t'
mak rum butter when thoo needs it." This implied that the
young woman would only have need of it when she had her
first child. It was regarded as 'not right' for a single woman to
make butter; it was rank heresy to make it for any other
reason than to celebrate a birth.

Since confinement, midwifery and admiring babies were
entirely feminine activities, the consumption of rum butter at
an accouchement also tended to be an all-female affair. As
time went on a method was devised which allowed the
menfolk a share of the delicacy.

This was called 'rum butter laitin', or 'sweet butter
stealing' which involved, as the name suggests, getting some
of the rum butter by fair means or foul. A special dish of rum
butter was made and hidden in the house where the baby was
born. Then a group of young men, with blackened faces to

hide their identify, some in female garb to make it easier to penetrate what was almost wholly female territory, entered the house and started their search. It was part of the pantomime that they were supposed to be either unrecognisable or invisible as they searched for and eventually found, the bowl of rum butter.

Then there was the problem of the few who had been inside the house dodging their friends who waited outside for their share of the feast. On one memorable night there was a 'stealing' at Bassenthwaite with six young men in the house and nearly sixty outside waiting in mouth-watering anxiety for them to emerge with their prize. But the 'laiters' sold them the dummy. The fastest runner of the gang set off out of the house with "T article wid a hannle on it frae under t' bed" hidden under a cloth. He drew the crowd, shed them when he discarded his "article wid a hannle", and then ran to join his friends in a barn for a feast of bread and rum butter.

Rum butter laitin lost its appeal in the Bassenthwaite area when the entire rigmarole was gone through, only for the stealers to discover that their prize was a bowl of oatmeal porridge with a thin skin of rum butter on the top.

Another of the rural pleasures enjoyed in the Cumberland of long ago was the 'taffy join', an occasion which developed over the ages to ensure that a steady marriage rate was maintained in the community.

There was in the taffy join something of the ceremonial, which hints at an origin in some pagan pairing ceremony. The toffee was made in the presence of the young people who were invited to the 'join'.

Joins were held by mothers of unmarried daughters with the object of getting the lasses off their hands before they finished up in that detestable harem of old maidism — on the shelf. How far the taffy join went in fulfilling its objective depended upon the good looks and the prospects of fortune of the young lady or ladies on offer, and not at all upon the quality or quantity of the taffy.

The mistress of the house made the toffee in a pan. This took time which was used by the young people in improving their acquaintance with one another, which was a vital part of the business on hand since the hostess had usually allocated partners for the girls, taking care to place her own daughters alongside the young men "wid t' maist brass", or with the best prospects of acquiring some.

There were, of course, drawbacks to the 'taffy join' system of match-making, the principal one being that sometimes it did not work at all. A particularly plain daughter of a somewhat desperate mother would find herself the cause of — and the central figure at — several taffy joins, with her male guests diminishing in wealth and prospects as they ran through to the fag end of the eligible males, and eventually into a situation when neither the girl nor her mother would have what was left of the marriageable males.

Even the taffy join became commercial, and most communities had old ladies who would hold a join and charge a copper or two for admission. They usually gave good value, and the best thing about this sort of taffy join was that the lads could choose their own partners. There was comfort in these 'paid' joins for the mothers of daughters who knew that if romance was likely to bud at one of them, it was at least happening in the presence of a chaperone.

Entertainment was a necessity at a boon ploughing as a means of repaying the generosity of neighbours who brought their ploughs to give a newcomer a good start with the work on his land. The same could be said of a clay daubin' which belonged to a more distant age when ground rents were peppercorns, and all that was required to build a house was a numerous company of willing neighbours. Everybody mucked in, literally. They puddled the clay and mixed it with straw and daubed it on a wattle frame or built solid clay walls until the house was finished, and then there was the usual food and drink and dance and games. In the district between Wigton and Abbey Town some clay-built houses are still in use.

Sheep clipping was another communal activity, and some clippings were famous for the hospitality offered when the last fleece had been tied, principal among them being the Nelsons of Gatesgarth and the Tysons of Gillerthwaite in Ennerdale. It must have been lavish hospitality which would lure a man a dozen miles to spend a day "up to t' neck in ruddle an' soave, an' hoaf worrit be sheep tyadds" for no

Crummock Water

Derwentwater from Brandlehow

'Camp Six' of the early Borrowdale explorers: the church at Stonethwaite

other reward. 'Ruddle' was the red dye used for marking sheep. 'Soave' was sheep salve which had an abominable smell; and 'tyadds' were the ticks with which sheep were infested.

Clippings usually had all the womenfolk at work as well preparing and serving the food and drink, and when all was over there would be running and wrestling, the prizes usually being fleeces of wool. Then there would be a dance for the young while the older part of the company would elect a chairman and sing songs and tell tall stories while hot toddy and saucersfull of tobacco were handed round until all was blue with smoke.

Thirsty work, clipping! It was a punishing time for the drink and more often than not the tap was drawn from the ale cask and all the spirit bottles were standing upside down before the night was over. "Merry neets mak sad mwornin's" was as true for the festival of sheep clipping as for any of the other festivals held around the major events of rural Cumbria, and there were usually a lot of sore heads being carried along to the next day's clipping.

It was the same with the harvest; the same folk usually; the same sort of festivity when all had been gathered in.

Throughout the harvesting everybody looked forward to the 'kurn supper' which, though it marked the end of the harvesting, was in no sense a 'Harvest Home', which had a religious connotation. The kurn supper was preceded by the shearing out which, in turn was surrounded by sufficient ritual to suggest that this was another echo of pagan festivals.

It was deemed lucky to have the last cut of a harvest, and it was an honour to be competed for. As much corn was left standing as would make a handful for the sickle, and then the heads were tied together and the reapers would throw their sickles at it from a mark, the 'luck' going to the one who made the best shot and cut it down. After that everybody went to wash and prepare for supper of haver or barley bannocks (large, flat, round loaves of bread often cooked in a frying pan) and butter; cakes and butter sops, and ale and whisky galore. This was followed by dancing and cards.

But the last cut of corn still had a part to play. It was plaited into 'a fanciful shape', with a big, rosy apple in the middle of it. This was hung in the farmer's kitchen until Christmas Day when the farmer or his man came downstairs before the household was astir; took the apple and gave it to whomever was considered to be the nicest lass in the house, and then took the last cut of corn and gave it to the best cow in the byre.

It was not always the best way to start a Christmas day. The best cow in the byre never found any fault with the last cut; but the women about the farm did and many a farmer and farm man spent his Christmas morning learning, if he did not know already, that the fury of a woman scorned is indeed hell.

7

Heamly Dance, Teun, Teal or Sang

Cumbrians had, and many still have, a colourful dialect with which to express their feelings, but in the expression of high spirits the Cumbrians of old obviously believed that actions spoke louder than words, and nowhere more loudly than in the dance.

High spirits notwithstanding, there was an air of grim earnestness about the dancing as if it meant something, like an echo of a forgotten past when dancing was ceremonial rather than recreational. That the dance was important as a recreational pursuit in times remembered is shown by the many references to it in the local literature. It was physical rather than artistic, and seems to have consisted principally in either leaping to the ceiling or 'battering the floor' as at Phil the Fluter's Ball. To be a good dancer was a sort of status symbol for a man; not so important for a woman because they seem to have taken a secondary part in dances. Both Robert Anderson, the Cumberland Bard, and Blind John Stagg, the fiddler-poet, make much of men's dancing, but say little about the quality of the women's part.

In Anderson's epic "The Blackell Murry Neet", the star billing goes to:

> The clogger o' Dawston's a famish top hero,
> And bangs aw the player-fwoak twenty to yen;
> He stamped wid his fit, and he shouted and royster'd
> Till the sweat it ran off at his varra chin en';
> Then he held up a han' like the spout of a tea-pot;
> And danced 'cross the Buckle' and 'Leather te patch';
> When they cried 'Bonny Bell' he lap up to the ceilin',
> And aye cracked his thoums for a bit of a fratch.

The Dalston clogger's solo dance was surely the hit of the evening, and in his vivid description Anderson captures the effort which went into it. It makes believable the remark passed at a dance by a lovelorn girl about her love's performance on the dance floor: "He hes a terrible romantic way o' throwin' oot his feet."

The women danced in a less spectacular fashion, seldom allowing enthusiasm to overcome discretion. This was how it had to be because the women shared a problem with the true Scot whose cavorting in the kilt was, and maybe still is, inhibited by the fact that he wore nothing underneath.

Neither, apparently, did the countrywomen of bygone days. Thomas Farrall, historian and agriculturist as well as author of the dialect classic *Betty Wilson's Cummerlan' Teals* wrote, on the subject of dress:

> t' Fwoaks' driss wus comfortable an' substantial. T' maister wore rib, an' hed a sleeved waistcwoat, seah he cuid git up til a job uv wark in a second. T' lads followed his example. T' mistress and t' lasses hed bedgoons, blue petticwoats an' winsey skirts. Theer war neah drawers in them days, an' Ah mind when Jane Dodd got a pair, it was gossip'd aw ower t' neighbourhood 'at Jane Dodd hed gitten herself inter breeks.[1]

Farrall was writing in 1886 about life in Cumberland 'sixty eer sen', so that Jane Dodd's introduction of drawers to the local fashion scene can be dated about 1820. This could be the reason why the earlier dialect poets like Anderson and Stagg seldom had cause to mention women as dancers of any particular merit. Cumbrians seem to have had few inhibitions when the ale was flowing, but they drew the line at allowing the women folk to make exhibitions of themselves.

Not always were the women left out. Mark Lonsdale (1758-1815) another Cumberland dialect poet, who became manager of Sadler's Wells, wrote an all-action piece called "The Upshot", about an Orton Merry Night in which drinking and eating, singing and carding, the maskers[3] and dancing were all included, and in lively style pictures a robust, roystering night, with the women participating in no uncertain manner:

> By neens at yence they fell to wark
> Wi' 'Jenny dang the weaver',
> Wheyle Worton lads were lowpin' man,
> An' shoutit 'Yoicks to Cleaver!'
>
> Tom Leytle, wid a fearful' bree,
> Gat hoald o' Dinah Glaister —
> She danc't a famish jig, an' he
> Was Thursby dancing maister.
> But just as Leytle gev a spang
> Leyke a feyne squoaverin' callan,
> Loft boards they brack, an' theer he stack
> A striddlin' cock'd o' th' hallan.
>
> Lang Cowper Watt sae whang't about
> He made Nan Boustead dizzy,
> An' then set up a roughsome shout,
> 'Seye! Seye! to the druck'n hizzy!'
> Says gunner Bell to Brandy Matt,
> 'Damme! but I's in order!
> Play up, auld chiel', a rantin't reel —
> Whoop! hey for 'Watt o' the bworder.' "

Lonsdale, Stagg and Anderson were all contemporary with Wordsworth who, whilst admittedly living in a different world, and painting the Lake Country and its people in the colours he thought best suited the good, honest, moral society in which he imagined he saw them, did admit to their letting their hair down at times, and in "The Waggoner" writes of:

> Blithe souls and lightsome hearts have we
> Feasting at The Cherry Tree.

The *Cherry Tree* was the 'other', older inn at Wythburn by Thirlmere, the more famous one being the *Nag's Head*, across the road from Wythburn Church, and it was certainly with first-hand experience of the occasion that he wrote:

> What bustling — jostling — high and low!
> A universal overflow!
> What tankards foaming at the tap!
> What thumping, stumping overhead!
> With such a stir you would have said,
> This little place may well be dizzy!

'Tis who can dance with greatest vigour —
'Tis what can be most prompt and eager;
As if it heard the fiddle's call,
The pewter clatters on the wall;
The very bacon shows its feeling,
Swinging from the smoky ceiling!

Joseph Palmer, who discovered the Beauty of Buttermere, recorded an incident at a dance he attended at Mary Robinson's home, the Fish Inn, Buttermere, which adequately describes the untrammelled way in which the dalesfolk took their amusement. Palmer wrote:

> A stout man, more than six feet, belonging to Lorton, entered, and most piteously regretted that he had not known of the dance as his iron-bound clogs were too heavy to dance in. Mine being by this time dry, I offered to lend him them for the night, but he had the disappointment to find them too short, for he said: 'They wad hae dinn varra weel', though, by the by, they weighed 2 pounds 7 ounces.
> However, he was soon among the dancers, and footed it away in his stockinged feet, and they were worn out, barefooted.

Such dedication to the dance seems not to have been uncommon. What sort of dancing it was is not easy to discover because all the remains of it is names of some of the dances and broad outlines of what the dancers did, and though it was mainly a pastime in which everyone participated, it seemed to have occasions when it became a spectator pastime.

Some of the dancing was highly individual stuff, like the Clogger of Dalston's contribution to the Blackhall Merry Night, and there were certainly some outstanding solo performers. Sometimes the dance was a double act as in the jigs in which two dancers, usually both men, would take the floor and dance their steps facing each other, each one trying to outlast the other.

Anderson gives the names of some of the dances, or, since dancing seems to have been left to the ability of inventiveness of the dancer, the tunes. There is "Cross the Buckle", "Leather to Patch" and "Bonny Bell". Mark Lonsdale mentions "Jenny dang the weaver", and Auld Hoggart of Troutbeck (Windermere) in a dialogue song called "Mopsus and Marina" writes of "Roundelayes", "Irish Hayes", "Cogs and Rongs", "Peggy Ramsey", "Spanaleto", "The Veneto", "Wilson's Fancy" and "John come kiss me" . . .

> But of all there's none so sprightly
> To my ears as 'Touch me lightly.'

In some dancing the object was to stamp the feet on the floor as hard as could be, as shown in Wordsworth's description of the Merry Night at the *Cherry Tree*, Wythburn, and in the example set by Tom Leytle, the Thursby dancing master in Lonsdale's "The Upshot" who leaped and stamped so hard that he went through the floorboards of the loft and landed, painfully, astride the beam.

The fiddler was the most important person in any activity where dancing was concerned and his only rival in the art of music making was the fluter.

'Blin' Stagg made very little money out of his poems, but managed to scrape (literally) a living out of his fiddling, and as a popular fiddler was a man of some consequence. Jonathan Brammery, who rates a mention from Lonsdale, but only as being inferior at his trade to Stagg, was a butt to all who met him and his fiddling was more notable for its tempo than its tune, he being a "sore tormentor of catgut".

Occasionally the fiddler blended his musical occupation with another as dancing master, which gave him two bites at anything to be made out of the entertainment business of those days by charging for lessons — or for regular dances at which he gave lessons — and being paid on other social occasions when his dancing lessons were put into practice. The dancing master-fiddler played his fiddle and called the moves as in western square dancing today; sometimes he just played for the reels and jigs any tune that was called.

One of the best known characters who combined the jobs of fiddler and dancing master was Ben Wells of Beckermet whose fame was widespread throughout Cumberland. "As taught by Ben Wells, dancing was something in which vigour, activity and precision were, rather than gracefulness, the main desiderata," wrote Alexander Craig Gibson in his *Folk Speech of Cumberland and the Counties Adjacent.*[4]

The dances, as taught by Ben Wells were intricate and required skill and a good memory for the moves and steps. These had to be performed correctly at the dances at which Ben played because he considered every public dance was a continuation of the last lesson he gave, and the dancers were careful not to put a foot wrong lest he stop the dancing and put it right.

Thomas Farrall told the story of Ben Jobson who gave dancing lessons to the girls of a boarding school for half a crown a session. This was in the first half of the nineteenth century, and suggests that dancing as taught by fiddlers was moving up the social scale. His fiddle, Ben claimed, had charmed the heart of man and soothed a savage beast. He was no doubt a good fiddler, which accounts for the 'charming'; his soothing of a savage beast referred to an occasion when, confronted by a savage dog, he took his fiddle out of its green baize bag and drew from it such terrible shrieks that the bewildered dog tucked its tail between its legs and ran off.

Ben Wells was the subject of one of Craig Gibson's beter dialect poems, but Gibson sheds more light on Ben in his preface than in the actual poem:

> As a violin player his performance was remarkably correct, distinct, and strongly marked as to time — in fact the best possible fiddling to dance to.
>
> The last time I met him was about the year 1848 in a bar parlour of an inn in the southern part of the Lake District, which was somewhat outside his ordinary beat, and where the strains of his fiddle, produced at my request, caused such excitement that a general and uproarious dance (of males only) set in, and was kept up with such energy that, the space being confined, the furniture was seriously damaged, and Ben was at last ejected by the landlady as the readiest, indeed the only method of putting a stop to the riot.
>
> He was light, muscular and springy, and in his younger days wonderfully swift of foot so much so that the late Dr. Johnstone, of Cockermouth, told me that he once, at Scale Hill, saw him, without assistance, run and catch a rabbit — proof of activity rarely parallelled.

In Gibson's poem about Benn Wells, one verse goes:

> Ben Wales's fiddle, many a neet,
> Gev weel oiled springs to t' heaviest heels,
> For few cud whyet hod the'r feet
> When Ben strack up his heartenin' reels.
> Wid elbow room an' rozel'd weel,
> Swinge! How he'd mak fwoke keav an' prance;
> An' nowt cud match t' sly fiddle squeal
> 'At signalled t' kiss i' t' cushion dance.

The cushion dance was the best loved and most important dance of any night for this was the dance at which partners for the homeward ride or trek were chosen. The men picked up cushions and danced around holding it with both hands until the music stopped and then knelt on the floor and put the cushion down in front of the girl who was expected to kneel on it and kiss the man who brought it.

Sometimes, to make things more confusing and to upset the mental form-books already quoting odds in the minds of local gossips, the cushion dance became a 'ladies' choice', the girls having the cushions and choosing the men to kiss.

But kissing was not always confined to the cushion dance, and in "The Waggoner" Wordsworth makes reference to the custom whereby "at the close of each strathspey or jig, a particular note from the fiddle summons the rustic to the agreeable duty of saluting his partner."

> With bowl that spread from hand to hand,
> The gladdest of the gladsome band,
> Amid their own delight and fun,
> They hear — when every dance is done,
> When every whirling bout is o'er —
> The fiddle's squeak — that call to bliss,
> Ever followed by a kiss."

Dancing in the old style continued into the twentieth century in some places, but in the second half of the nineteenth century 'modern' dancing was already catching on.

Canon Rawnsley, in the very early nineteen hundreds could write of the funeral of a fiddler named "Dick o' the Dale", and remember:

"Not a farm around
But knew of the sound
Of the wavering voice and the quavering fiddle;
Not a man nor maid
But had danced as he played,
'Set to corners' and then 'down the middle.' "

The cushion dance apparently went 'oot o' vogue' when Ben Wells was laid to rest, and a wind of change began to blow over the dancing scene in the Lake Country as new people, new ideas for leisure, new dances, new social structures began to take over from the old.

Perhaps it was because the natural reserve of the Cumbrian, in the company of strangers, drew the line at giving the freedom of the kissing cushion to offcomers that it went out of fashion. But it did go out of fashion and so did the other dances, and so also did the fiddler disappear from the Lakeland scene, and things would never be the same again. As Gibson wrote in his personal tribute to Ben Wells:

Fwoake's ways turn different, t' langer t' mair,
An' what, lang sen, was reet's grown wrang;
We're meast on us, owre fine to care
For heamly dance, teun, teal, or sang.[5]
An' nowt's mead varra lastin' here;
T' best bow hand growes oald an' fails,
An' t' lishest legs git num an' queer;
Few last sa weel as oald Ben Wales.

8

A Large Piece of Lawless Patchwork

Wordsworth wandered lonely as a cloud in the best known of his poems; he has been accused of sitting tight on his passing cloud and omitting to get down to the grass roots of life in the Lake Country.

On only one occasion, as far as can be ascertained, did he perch himself upon a hypothetical cloud and admit to taking a downward and distant view of his favourite part of the world. "Let us suppose," he wrote in his *Guide to the Lakes*, "our station to be a cloud hanging midway between those two mountains [Great Gable and Scawfell] . . . we shall then see stretched at our feet a number of valleys, not fewer than eight, diverging from the point on which we are supposed to stand like spokes from the nave of a wheel . . ."

A happy choice of viewpoint, if it could be available; but be thankful that between them the summits of both Gable and Scawfell offer all that Wordsworth described in his inimitable and invaluable guide. This is his view of Wasdale: " . . . little chapel and half a dozen neat dwellings scattered upon a plain of meadow and cornground intersected with stone walls apparently innumerable, like a large piece of lawless patchwork, or an array of mathematical figures, such as in the ancient schools of geometry might have been sportively and fantastically traced out upon sand." There is no other valley which presents such an intricate pattern of fields.

In his guide of 1819, Green wrote: "Wastdale Head is a narrow but fruitful vale, and if ridden of its stone walls, and more profusely planted, would truly be a postoral paradise." The walls which Green found too numerous are in themselves a tribute to generations of dalesmen who cleared them off the land and out of the soil in the form of boulders and hard-edged chips of rock brought down by glacier and water from the fells around. Stony soil this must indeed have been because there are corners of those patchwork fields which have been filled in with masses of stone which the tillers of the soil found long after the need for more walls had passed. The strangest thing about the Wasdale Head walls is that anybody was ever able to make any sense out of them; to sort out which field belonged to whom, and it would be most interesting to learn if this jigsaw pattern of ploughland and pasture ever had names to distinguish one patch from another.

Wasdale Head has been visited by outsiders from the early days when the death-or-glory boys who contributed articles to *Blackwoods* or the *Gentleman's Magazine* decided that it might be of some interest to see what was on the other side of the hill.

They came in a steady stream, to see Wastwater and its quickly famous screes, to visit the tiny chapel, to see Auld Will Ritson and listen to his outrageous tales; or just to say they had been there.

People also came for the climbing because for the rock climbers Wasdale Head was the jumping-off place for all that was best in that heady pastime.

One visitor was Dr David Ross Lietch, of Keswick, who travelled by pony over Sty Head on a "delicious" day in 1854. Dr Lietch and his companion led their horses down the steepest parts into Wasdale where, a few years before, Sir Charles Napier, hero of Corunna and India endeavouring to continue in the hero image, had galloped madly down, much to the horror of his guide.

Like almost everybody else, Wordsworth included, Leitch was taken by "the old quaint little chapel of Wasdale Head, one of the most truly picturesque in the hills. . . . sinking into the earth with humility and age, its single bell in its mouldering little turret overtopping the roof within reach of a tall man's arm." The chapel once had a clerk called Birkett who was obviously not tall enough to reach the bell because Auld Will Ritson told of an occasion when the parson came up for the morning service to find Birkett sitting astride the roof ringing the bell with a hammer, making up for the lack of a bell-rope which he had lent a local farmer to tie his hay-cart.

Lietch was impressed as much by the school as by the chapel. "Without doubt the smallest in England," he called it: a tiny building standing by itself with a stone-paved floor, a dozen pupils, and the last whittlegate dominie of the dales — and a schoolmaster whose salary was so small that it was eked out with free board and lodging in the homes of his pupils. The dozen children amply filled the school, half of them with the dark eyes of the Celt, half with the blue eyes of the Norse, but all equally grateful for the penny apiece the doctor left them.

Another visitor to this miniature school, still standing, and in danger sometimes of being turned into toilets for visitors to the dale, was Canon Rawnsley who, on an historic occasion in 1905, went there to present the school with a trophy awarded by the Cumberland Education Committee for the best attendance record for the year. With only nine pupils, perhaps Wasdale Head stood a better chance of attaining a 100 per cent attendance for a year, but it had the additional handicaps of atrocious winter weather and a catchment area extending 2½ miles. "It was heroic," said the Canon, describing the efforts of the parents of the five Roper children, which included the father loading all five up on a farm cart to take them to school on a wet day, and the mother sitting up all one night ladling spoonsful of black-berry syrup into the children to hasten them over the worst of a crop of colds.

Wasdale Head has had more than its share of even more distinguished visitors, almost all welcomed with typical dales hospitality. One of the lower key welcomes was laid on in 1915 for what the local newspaper correspondent called "some distinguished Socialists, Mrs Sydney Webb and Mrs George Bernard Shaw, accompanied by their husbands."

What the great G.B.S. and Sydney Webb thought of the dale's cool reception is not recorded but the village corres-pondent noted that these eminent Socialists did have a fine motor car with them which they did not place at the disposal of the local inhabitants while they were not using it, thus, according to this correspondent, violating one of the tenets of Socialism, as he saw it, of sharing their all with everybody else. "It is well known," he added, "that motor cars and pigs are special kinds of personal property to which Socialism does not apply."

A respected, even beloved, visitor to Wasdale Head was John Wilson, known best in the world of literature as 'Christopher North', first editor of *Blackwood's* magazine. Professor Wilson (he was professor of moral philosophy at Edinburgh) was a tough, athletic character, rejoicing in practical jokes, but at the same time a kindly, likeable man, and he struck up a friendship with Will Ritson in whom he found a fellow spirit, despite a twenty-year difference in their ages, Ritson being the younger. At the time Will was keeping the inn at Wasdale Head with his wife Dinah as hostess. He himself became as much an attraction for visitors as the fells around because his reputation for telling tall stories had spread sufficiently for him to be classed among the head's list of superlatives — the biggest liar, along with the deepest lake and the highest mountain. Liar he certainly was not, or at any rate he would not admit that his tales were anything but a slight stretching of the truth, mostly by popular demand and for popular entertainment.

But the tag 'biggest liar' did not always suit him; he tended to get impatient with people who persisted in so describing him. On one occasion a visitor was begging Will to tell some stories, but Will was not in the mood. The visitor persisted until Ritson, tired of his importuning, turned on him, looked him straight in the eye, and said: "Reet. Thoo wants a greet lee. Ah'll tell the t' biggest lee Ah've ivver tell't . . . Thoo's t' handsomest feller Ah've ivver seen."

In a lighter mood on the same subject, Will is said to have abdicated the title to a visiting bishop who said that he had never told a lie in his life.

Another time when he lost patience with visiting southerners anxious to hear his 'lies' he explained why there were fat trout in the stream behind his inn. "It's these fwoak frae Lunnon," he explained, "they come here lousy as sheep afoor soavin', an' they dook in t' beck, an' t' fish feed on what's weshed off them."

On an outing with some fishermen to one of the local tarns, the fishermen complained that they were getting no bites. Will explained that that was because all the trout were at the other side of the tarn, and sent half the party over to the other side to thrash the water with their sticks and chase the trout over to their friends. He told tales of big turnips: one so big that a bullock ate its way into it and was lost for some time; of big potatoes, so big that the grower refused to cut into one of them to serve a friend with a stone's weight. But only when he was in lighthearted mood, as when he guided a visiting cleric to the top of Scawfell and told him: "Tha'll nivver be nighter t' Heaven than noo."

Like many dalesmen of his time Ritson had a passion for hunting, having been huntsman for Mr Rawson of Wasdale Hall and Mr Huddleston of Gosforth, and he even tried forming a pack of his own; he always kept in touch with the farming scene being a regular attender at cattle and sheep sales and shows.

In his youth he was a wrestler of some note, and he had not quite passed his prime when he had his famous wrestling match with Professor Wilson winning two falls out of three, and then modestly explaining that his opponent was twenty years older and had walked 40 miles before the bout. "Not," he added, "that forty miles tewd [tired] him, for Ah've known him tramp seventy an' put in six hours fishing forbye in t' 24 hours."

Ritson was born in 1808 at Row Foot at the other end of the dale, retired in old age to a house at the foot of Buckbarrow, and died in 1890. The only photograph that is known to have been taken of him shows a long, lined face, mouth set tight obviously in an effort to obey the camera-man and keep still, but a mouth that could utter outrageous things without moving a muscle.

He had some women guests at the inn and one evening was regaling them with stories about the district, for once in serious mood, and he told them the story of the family — father, mother and six children — who set off over the Sty when a cloudburst hit them, a not too uncommon occurrence in the centre of Lakeland. Sorrowfully, Will told how in their anxiety to return home they waded into the raging water and how they were all swept away and drowned.

The guests, quietened by this unfolding of a tale of tragedy, remained silent at the end of the story, the silence only being broken by Will saying: "Ah weel. It might ha' been worse."

"Worse!" exclaimed one of the women.

"Ay," said Will, "it might ha' been true."

There are traditions of very early Christianity having come to the head of this wild dale, and that until comparatively recent times there were vestiges of the Celtic Church in the services at the little chapel. It is said that the chapel started as a cell for a monk of St Bees, but the date of its foundation is unknown, as is its dedication. It was there, however, at the Reformation because among its possessions is a communion cup of 1571, one of a large number of Elizabethan cups which materialised throughout this isolated area in that year on the order of Richard Barnes, Bishop of Carlisle.

Apparently the Reformation was having some difficulty in operating in this remote diocese. Barnes's predecessor, John Best, the first Protestant Bishop of Carlisle seems to have had quite enough to do without conducting a campaign against "massing chalices and other monuments of superstition." Queen Elizabeth empowered him to arm himself and his dependents against "the tumultuous and enraged populace", an indication that the transition to Protestantism was not exactly smooth in this region.

However, Bishop Barnes received from Archbishop Grindal of York who, incidentally, was a Cumbrian, having been born either at St Bees or Hensingham) an injunction for the substitution of 'cups' for 'chalices', an order which Bishop Barnes followed to the letter.

The huge, curved timber members of the roof supports of Wasdale Head Church have led some to suppose that they came originally from ships, a supposition to which some weight is given by the fact that Ravenglass once had a thriving industry in the breaking up of wooden ships. Close examination, however, will show that the oak timbers of this little church were cut and trimmed for the purpose they now fulfil.

In 1887 the population of Wasdale Head Parish was

forty-six, and the accommodation in the church was for fifty. In earlier days the capacity was probably less because the body of the church included six great box pews for the dale's more prominent families. Behind the communion rail is a piece of panelling which once formed the end of one of these box pews.

The tiny church, seeming to be sinking slowly into the ground under the weight of the massive slates and timbers which form its roof, was very much the centre of things in the dale. Almost everything stopped on Sunday for the church service, but everything was geared to go into action as soon as the last prayer was said, and farmers and their servants went to church in their working clothes if some urgent farm work was being attended to, and they kept their dogs tethered outside ready for work on the fell. On one memorable occasion a shepherd, diligent at his work, but delinquent of his duty to attend church, popped his head into the church in the middle of the sermon and called out: "Hes enny on you seen owt of an auld black yow an' a lamb on t' fell?"

One of the truly great families of Cumberland stemmed from Wasdale Head. One of the three landowners there in 1882 was a Fletcher, the family property deriving from an inheritance dating back to Norman times. One of the Fletchers, Henry, was host to Mary Queen of Scots when she slept in his Cockermouth Hall home in 1568 after her flight into Cumberland following defeat at the battle of Langside. From a beginning as a mercer he started a family line which included Fletcher Christian, and whose members owned such imposing residences as Hutton-in-the-Forest (still the family headquarters with Lord Inglewood at the head), Tallentire Hall and Moresby Hall.

Next to the church, the oldest man-made thing at Wasdale Head is the packhorse bridge behind the hotel which carries the track into Mosedale. Perhaps it was Will Ritson's penchant for exaggeration which gave it the name 'Roman' Bridge, for it is no older than any of the many similar bridges which still exist in the Lake Country, but its mere existence, like that of its cousins Stockley Bridge and Watendlath "nowhere and leading to everywhere", shows that the

Mosedale track was once an important packhorse route, a fact which is difficult to assimilate even at the height of summer these days when Black Sail Pass carries its maximum in leg-borne traffic between Wasdale and Ennerdale.

Down to the left from the Mosedale track is a haystack-size boulder the colour of which seems strangely pale, and a close examination will show that the pale parts are the scratches made by hundreds of climbing boots over the years when the ring clinker and tricouni reigned supreme as climbing aids, and the 'Vibrum' sole had not been invented. This is the 'Y' Boulder, so named because of the Y-shaped crack which splits it, a practice boulder for generations of rock climbers who, quite often, have found on it problems of a complexity sufficient to use up time which could be more satisfyingly used contending with the problems on Pillar.

9

Will the Real
Betty Yewdale . . .?

Wordsworth discovered Betty Yewdale. He put her into *The Excursion* in the role of one of the noble natives with which he peopled his Lakeland.

Whether in a spirit of simple curiosity; with a view to contradicting Wordsworth's view of Lake Country people (or this particular person), or holding him up to mild ridicule, Robert Southey sent out a fact-finding mission to, as modern newspapers would put it, 'probe' this Lakeland woman's background. However, since it does not seem to have been in Southey's nature to hurt anybody, it can be assumed that he just wished to find out more about Betty Yewdale. The fact that his investigators were Sarah Hutchinson, Wordsworth's sister-in-law, and Edith May Warter, his (Southey's) daughter, seems further to show that whatever the object of the exercise, it was not to set any slight on Wordsworth.

The meeting of Betty Yewdale, in old age, with Miss Hutchinson and Mrs Warter, did, however, produce a somewhat different picture from that Wordsworth had drawn. It also resulted in a dialect classic, recorded in the dialect Betty used, and published by Southey in "The Doctor".

Canon Rawnsley gave Betty Yewdale a brief mention in his "By Fell and Dale" but only because she found a novel use for the 'hogg-whoals' (holes to allow the passage of sheep from field to field) in the dry-stone walls which surround the fellside fields.

Alexander Craig Gibson who went to doctor the people in Coniston and Langdale did dig deeply for his posthumous examination of Betty Yewdale's character. As a writer of dialect which concentrated on the humorous, he liked what he found. As a critic of Wordsworth's high-flown view of

Lakeland and its people, he took a slightly malicious delight
in presenting her "in not quite so romantic a light" as
Wordsworth had in *The Excursion.*

Betty Yewdale won a place in the literature of the Lake
Country through Wordsworth and Southey, and she is firmly
established in the folklore not only of the Lakes, but also of
the Western Dales of Yorkshire.

But Wordsworth saw her first. If he had not encountered
her and produced a rather romanticised version of her in *The
Excursion* there would have been no cause for any further
examination of her, and Betty Yewdale would have gone to
her rest unknown, unremembered.

Wordsworth met Betty Yewdale some time in her middle
age. Yewdale was her married name, and though it is so
recorded by everybody who mentions her, it is quite likely
that the name would be 'Youdell', which is a name fairly
common still in the Langdales.

He met Betty in circumstances which could be described as
dramatic by stretching the imagination a little. But Wordsworth's imagination soared to produce a picture of life on the
lower stratum of Lake Country society which, though too
over-drawn for some to accept it without a quibble, at least
measured up to the view he held of the honest and humble
toilers in the wilds of Lakeland.

In Book Five ("The Pastor") of *The Excursion*, Wordsworth has his wanderer meeting the Pastor who tells him
about some of the people living among the mountains,
drawing particular attention to a spot.

> High on the breast of yon dark mountain, dark
> With stony barrenness, a shining speck
> Bright as a sunbeam sleeping till a shower
> Brush it away, or a cloud pass over it;
> And such it might be deemed — a sleeping sunbeam;
> But 'tis a plot of cultivated ground, cut off
> Cut off, an island in the dusky waste;
> And that attractive brightness is its own.

This plot of cultivated ground; this island in the dusky waste
is Hacket, above Elterwater a smallholding hacked out of the
fellside where live

A wedded pair in childless solitude.
A house of stones collected on the spot,
By rude hands built, with rocky knolls in front,
Backed also by a ledge of rock, whose crest
Of birch trees waves above the chimney top.
A rough abode — in colour, shape and size,
Such as in unsafe times of border war
Might have been wished for and contrived to elude
The eye of the roving plunderer.

The wedded pair in childless solitude are Betty and her husband, Jonathan Yewdale. They lived there for many years, and had been there for some time when Wordsworth first encountered them, Jonathan eking out a poor living from the smallholding by working in the quarries of Little Langdale.

Topographically, Wordsworth cannot be faulted. His description of Hacket then fits Hacket today perfectly. The house has been 'fettled up' like so many more of Lakeland's humble dwellings which have become 'second homes', but rocky knolls still dot the field in front of the house; a fringe of trees still decorates the crest of the rock against which the house is perched.

Hacket is the perfect retreat; such a house as might have been built, as Wordsworth suggests "to elude the eye of the roving plunderer". The field in front of the house can still appear a shining speck, bright as a sunbeam, from the other side of Little Langdale, which, presumably, was Wordsworth's viewpoint.

In childless solitude the couple lived, but Betty found some fulfilment in caring for their little plot of land while her husband grafted in the quarries. Wordsworth's Pastor tells her story to the Wanderer:

she beguiles
By intermingled work of house and field
The summer's day, and winter's; with success
Not equal, but sufficient to maintain,
Even at the worst, a smooth stream of content,
Until the expected hour at which her mate
From the far-distanct quarry's vault returns;
And by his converse crowns a silent day
With evening cheerfulness.

The Pastor has not yet finished his eulogy on this pair living their idyllic life among the mountains, and the poet drives relentlessly on to have the Pastor complete it with that secret ingredient, humility:

> in powers of mind,
> In scale of culture, few among my flock
> Hold lower rank than this sequestered pair;
> But true humility descends from Heaven;
> And that best gift of Heaven hath fallen upon them;
> Abundant recompense for every want.

The Pastor's picture is complete, but there is yet a moral to be pointed:

> Stoop from your height, ye proud, and copy these;
> Who in their noiseless dwelling place can hear
> The Voice of Wisdom whispering Scripture texts
> For the mind's government, or temper's peace;
> And recommending for their mutual need,
> Forgiveness, patience, hope, and charity.

A voice whispering Scripture texts for temper's peace and recommending forgiveness, patience, hope and charity — this is not Wordsworth's idealizing imagination working overtime, for the temper to be appeased, sins to be forgiven, and patience to be exercised hint at trouble in the home, discord around the fireside.

So the poem continues, the wanderer, apparently unable to get a word in edgeways while the Pastor was delivering his discourse upon the inhabitants of Hacket, eventually reveals that he had already encountered this couple on a previous expedition, and adds a few touches to the picture of domestic serenity the Pastor has painted. The Wanderer tells that once he was traversing the mountains when the dark autumnal evening fell, and, feeling his way cautiously along the fellside, he saw a light, high in the gloom "too high, methought, for human habitation". With nothing else to guide him, he went towards the light, and when he got there found it was held by a woman who was out there to guide her husband home from the distant quarry.

Jonathan's homeward trek led through Little Langdale and along the green path which still exists as an accommodation road (it is not a public right of way) and which winds up the fellside to Hacket which, in its eyrie-like site, is invisible until one is right upon it.

Disappointed at first, and alarmed, when she found that the man she had attracted by her light was not her husband, the woman recovered, and, because hospitality always came before self-interest — or a husband who might get lost in the dark — she invited the Wanderer to the house:

> 'But come
> Come,' said the matron, 'to our poor abode;
> Those dark rocks hide it.

The Wanderer is welcomed to a blazing fire beside a cleanly hearth, and then the dame excuses herself to return to her watch outside with her swinging lantern.

Before the cottage fire, "a glowing pile of mountain turf", required any attention, she was back with her husband. There followed hospitable fare, and "frank conversation which made the evening's treat" — and an opportunity for the Wanderer to examine the husband. He is struck by

> the good man's form and face
> Not less than beautiful; an open brow
> Of undisturbed humanity; a cheek
> Suffused with something of a feminine hue;
> Eyes beaming courtesy and mild regard;
> But in the quicker turns of their discourse,
> Expression slowly varying, that evinced
> A tardy apprehension.

Even if the term had been in use at the time, Wordsworth would not have demeaned himself or his subject by saying that Jonathan Yewdale was a bit dim. In the local idiom Jonathan would be called by his contemporaries 'short o' leet', 'nick'd at t' heed', or 'hofe thick'.

Wordsworth's description of him, even if it did not descend to the home truths of the locals, was not far from the truth of the matter. Jonathan was a simple, gentle soul, in appearance almost too good to be true. Of him, Southey was to write in "The Doctor": "He was a perfect picture, like those we meet in the better copies of the Saints in our old Prayer Books."

But what had happened to the Jonathan the Pastor found
on his visit to Hacket; the man who, returning from his work
in the quarry

> by his converse crowns a silent day
> With evening cheerfulness?

Wordsworth probably went more than once to Hacket,
and, without specifically mentioning it, found a change in the
atmosphere, or at least in Jonathan's demeanour, for,
according to the Wanderer the man of the house took little
part, if any, in the evening's conversation. At any rate,
nothing he said is recorded.

Betty, however, has plenty to say about her lonely lot at
Hacket:

> Three dark mid-winter months
> Pass, and I never see,
> Save when the Sabbath brings it kind release,
> My helpmate's face by light of day. He quits
> His door in darkness, nor till dusk returns,
> And through Heaven's blessing, thus we gain the bread
> For which we pray.

That is how Wordsworth put it. Betty almost certainly said
something like: "Ah nivver see him by daylest frae ya
week-end tull anudder." What else she said in her native
tongue would make very interesting reading for a lover of
dialect, and so would the rest of her conversation in which
she details the compensations in her lonely life: her com-
panions, dependents, friends, comforters:

> my wheel, my fire,
> All day the house-clock ticking in mine ear,
> The cackling hen, the tender chicken brood,
> And the wild birds that gather round my porch,
> The honest sheep-dog's countenance I read;
> With him can talk; nor blush to waste a word
> On creatures less intelligent and shrewd.
> And if the blustering wind that drives the clouds
> Care not for me, he lingers round my door
> And makes the pastime when our tempers suit; —
> But, above all, my thoughts are my support,

My comfort; — would that they were oftener fixed
On what, for guidance in the way that leads
To Heaven, I know, by my Redeemer taught.

Such were the privations, and the compensations, of a
humble, isolated life in Langdale long ago. The nearest house
was nearly a mile away, and there was Betty busying herself
about the house, with the poultry and other stock and her
spinning wheel, talking quietly to herself, to the understanding dog, to the birds.

Wordsworth completes the picture, squeezing the last drop
of sentiment from this idyll of the Langdales:

Oh happy! Yielding to the law
Of these privations, richer in the main! —
While thankless thousands are opprest and clogged
By ease and leisure
For you the hours of labour do not flag;
For you each evening hath its shining star,
And every Sabbath-day its golden sun.

A splendid old couple taking the rough of fellside life in
the Langdales a century and a half ago with the smooth, even
if the smooth came but rarely, and briefly, after Betty's
shining star had successfully guided Jonathan home in the
evening, or on a Sunday when he did not have to go to work
at all. They seem to have impressed Wordsworth as being, in
the main, contented with their lot. "Be thankful for small
mercies" seems to have been the theme of their lives.
Jonathan's early life is a mystery, but at least one incident in
Betty's life is well documented; an incident which shows that
life in the Lakeland dales was not so idyllic after all.

Langdale-born — she called it 'Langden' as all the other
natives did, and still do — Betty was the daughter of a farm
worker who also had a smallholding. He also had a surplus of
daughters, certainly more of them than were required at
home, for when Betty was between seven and eight years old,
she and her sister Sally, two years younger, were sent to learn
a trade. Their parents probably never intended it that way,
but they fell for the sales talk of a woman of Dent in the
West Yorkshire dales just over the Border from Westmorland.
She met Betty's parents, a bargain was struck, and, there and

then Betty and Sally were handed over to the woman of Dent. All Betty said when she was telling the tale — which was recorded by Sarah Hutchinson and Edith May Warter and used by Southey in "The Doctor" under the title of "The Terrible Knitters e' Dent" — was: "They er terrible knitters e' Dent, an' Mudder an' Fadder sent me an' my lile sister back wi' her at larn at knit."

So Betty, aged 7, and Sally, aged 5, were sent to work among the knitters of Dent. Betty told her tale when she was about 65 and living at Rydal, and she recalled that she and her sister did not like Dent at all. It was not that they were ill-treated; but their way of living was rough. 'Way of living' to Betty meant, mainly, the food they ate. "It was round meal — an' they stoult it in t' frying pan, e' keaks as thick as my finger."

Betty and Sally soon became homesick, and when they were alone, they discussed ways and means of getting away from Dent.

It was between Christmas and Candlemas, the coldest time of the year, when their opportunity came. They could make no preparations because they were afraid of alerting the knitters, so they took off as they stood, in mid-winter through slushy snow wearing their clogs, hats, "blue bedgoons", which were standard apparel for women and girls, and "brats" (aprons). Betty had sixpence in her pocket; no more because they dare not touch the three or four shillings they had in a box at the 'knitters' which their parents had given them as pocket money.

Young and badly equipped for a mid-winter journey across country, the tiny couple were not without resource. After Betty had begged in vain for a bit of bread at a fine "girt reed hoose" near Sedbergh, she suggested that at the next house Sally, being the smaller, should beg. "Mappen they'll sarra [serve] us," she said. And they did, and gave the wandering mites "a girt shive of bread".

Three days later they roused their parents in the middle of the night "stannin' doddering, an' daized wi' cauld, as near dead as maks nae matter", their mother burst out crying, "an' we grat [wept] — an' my fadder grat an' aw, an' they dudden't flight [scold], nor said nought tull us for coming away."

The adventure was over. The terrible knitters of Dent

made no serious effort to secure the return of the runaways, and had, in fact, made no more than a token search for them the night they disappeared.

The story of "The Terrible Knitters e' Dent" seems to have been a bonus accruing from an investigation set afoot by Southey into the character Wordsworth produced in *The Excursion*. When Miss Hutchinson and Mrs Warter produced the story, Southey stored it away for use on some future occasion.

The occasion arose when Southey was compiling "The Doctor", and since dear old Doctor Dove was a man of many parts and many experiences, and since "The Doctor" seems to be an exercise in everything Southey knew or could do, it seems to fit comfortably in.[1]

But the record must be put straight on "The Terrible Knitters e' Dent." The word "terrible" in its normal usage, does fit Betty Yewdale's story of the knitters of Dentdale, and that Southey accepted their title in that sense is shown in his own comment that the story would be read "with interest by humane manufacturers, and by masters of spinning jennies with a smile".

Readers of the story can be excused for believing that the knitters of Dent were indeed terrible people, but Betty used the word in her story to Miss Hutchinson and Mrs Warter in the local idiom which turns 'terrible' from adjective into adverb.

Today a Herdwick farmer will describe his own strain of sheep as a 'terrible good breed', and a hound which leads the pack as a 'terrible good runner'. A man or girl can be a 'terrible good dancer', or the men who holds the chair in a pub discussion can be a 'terrible talker' or a 'terrible liar'.

Betty started off her tale by saying "They er terrible knitters e' Dent", and so provided a headline, and also bestowed a title which the people of Dentdale must have found difficult to live down. What Betty meant to say was that the knitters of Dent were 'terrible good', 'terrible keen' or 'terrible hard-working'.

From "The Terrible Knitters e' Dent" Betty emerges, at the tender age of 7, as a child of courage and resource which she drew upon to see herself and her little sister over that dreadful winter walk.

The woman Wordsworth met and wrote into *The Excursion* seems just the sort of woman the little adventurer would become: independent, courageous in the face of the discouragements and hard work of a fellside smallholding; prepared to stand out on that fellside on cold winter nights with a lantern to guide her less-than-perfect husband home.

It was to be expected that Betty, the little leader, would grow into a strong-willed woman. But there was another side to her character which Wordsworth missed, or ignored. In 1843 Dr Alexander Craig Gibson took over the practice at Coniston, his 'beat' including the Langdales. A poet himself of some little merit, and a student and writer of dialect, he was not a fanatical admirer of Wordsworth, saying that the great poet seemed unable to lower himself sufficiently from his lofty standpoint to be able to see at their own level the people of the Lake Country and the lives they led. Whilst applauding the quality of Wordsworth's writing, Gibson could not refrain from criticism of the poet's inability to come down from that passing cloud and get down to grass roots. And it was in critical mood that Gibson took an interest in the passage about the Yewdales in *The Excursion*.

Both Betty and Jonathan were dead and gone when Gibson arrived in the district, but there were 'Langden' folk who remembered them, and it was from these people that he obtained his information.

Writing about 1850 in *Folk Speech of Cumberland and Counties Adjacent* Gibson said he had discovered that Jonathan Yewdale had indeed "almost seraphic beauty" of features, "lowered, as it was, by a lack of expression, denoting a weakness of mind and character, which, in the opinion of neighbours, perfectly justified Betty in maintaining full domestic supremacy and undisputed rule."

So Gibson confirms Wordsworth's description of Jonathan's "face not less than beautiful" with "expression slowly varying, that evinced a tardy apprehension".

The pairing of Jonathan with Betty seems to have been a result of the atraction of opposites. Betty was described by those who knew her as "shrewd and masculine", and she needed somebody to dominate; Jonathan, a quiet, timid creature, needed somebody as a driving force. And 'driving' was, painfully for Jonathan, the operative word in one incident of their married life.

Gibson shed a different light upon Betty from that with which Wordsworth had illumined the woman on the fellside beside Hacket.

Everybody in the Langdales, and right down to Coniston, remembered the day Jonathan went to a funeral. The funeral was from Hall Garth, and, in the way of the time, as it still is in parts of Scotland, funerals were mainly men's business. Nearly all the men of Little Langdale went with the funeral to Coniston. No doubt that night Betty kept her usual vigil on the fellside to guide Jonathan home with her lantern. But Jonathan did not come home, and still had not turned up at breakfast time.

When there was still no sign of Jonathan after breakfast, Betty set off for Oxenfell where she asked the woman of the house, also in a state of grass widowhood: "Has yower meeaster gitten back fray t' funeral?" The Oxenfell wife replied that her man had not yet returned — and that she was not going to "lait" him. She knew her place, and at that time her place was at home, sitting and waiting patiently.

Waiting anxiously with a swinging lantern on the fellside for Jonathan returning from work was something entirely different from sitting patiently at home waiting for him to return in whatever condition he may have reached in the festivities which usually followed funerals. Deciding that patience, in this case, was no longer a virtue, Betty set off for Coniston.

Gibson paints a vivid picture of the couple returning to Hacket some hours later. The sight, for once, of "her helpmate's face by light of day" — or by what light could penetrate the smoke-charged and rum-reeking atmosphere of the Black Bull at Coniston — seems to have brought out the worst in her. Betty returned to Little Langdale, driving Jonathan before her with a good, switchy hazel stick. Let Gibson in the dialect of the Oxenfell wife, who told him the tale, describe the scene: "He sartly was a sairy object. His Sunda' cleeas leeuk't as if he'd been sleeping i' them on a durty flooer. T' tie of his neckcloth had work'd roon' till belaw ya lug, an' t' lang ends on't hung oo'er ahint his shoulder. His hat hed gitten bulg'd in at t' side, an' t' flipe [brim] on t' was cocked up beeath back an' front. O' t'gidder, it wod ha' been a queerly woman body 'at would ha' teean [taken] a fancy till Jonathan that day."

Betty landed like a hurricane in the midst of the men of Langdale gathered in the *Black Bull*. They were about to sit down to dinner when she arrived; a great pan of beefsteaks was already on the table. Betty sent the pan of steaks flying through the front door, and then gave the Langdale men a piece of her mind for keeping Jonathan away from home. Then she hauled her husband out from among them, and set off home.

But even in that state of mind, Betty had her pride, and had to consider what the neighbours might think. Jonathan was such a sight that she was ashamed to be seen on the road with him. So she took to the fields, driving Jonathan before her. And because he had taken drink, and was somewhat unsteady on his feet, she considered it unsafe to allow Jonathan to climb over the dry-stone walls. Instead, she made him creep through the hogg-holes. "An'," said Betty, when telling of the incident later, "when I gat him wi' his heead in an' his legs oot, I dud switch him."

In another version of the story which was told to Canon Rawnsley some years later and recorded in *By Fell and Dale*, Betty was asked by a neighbour how she had managed to get Jonathan home she replied: "I just threshed him through t' hogg-whoals."

How often Betty resorted to the hazel switch to keep Jonathan on the straight and narrow is not known. It was probably not very often, or this story would not have founds its way, as it has, into the folklore of Langdale. "This true story shows Wordsworth's humble heroine is not quite so romantic a light as he throws on her in the passage in *The Excursion*, Gibson points out, "but I don't see that it need lower her in our esteem."

Jonathan died before Betty, and she spent the last years of her life in a cottage at Rydal where she was living when she was visited by Sarah Hutchinson and Edith May Warter. At that time she was an old woman, "but with a bright black eye".

"A shrewd and masculine woman was Betty Yewdale," wrote Southey, "fond of the nicotine weed, and a short pipe so as to have the full flavour of its essence. Somewhat, sooth be said, too fond of it, for the pressure of the pipe produced a cancer in her mouth which caused her death."

10

Friends of the Floating Island

The tale with which travellers are amused, of a floating island, appears on strict examination to be fabulous.

Obviously William Hutchinson did not believe there was a floating island in Derwentwater; the quotation above comes from the 1794 edition of his *History of Cumberland*. Already wise to the wiles of the people of the Lake Country and the tall stories they told, he thought the floating island was something which had been invented for the amusement of the visitors: an eighteenth-century tourist trap.

But if Hutchinson was determined not to be 'taken in' by the natives over the floating island, he treated seriously of the 'bottom wind' of Derwentwater; and published in the most intricate detail the story of the ghost army of Souther Fell.

Scientific men were contemptuous of the so-called 'bottom wind' which they regarded merely as a disturbance of air natural in a hilly district. The only possible explanation of the ghost army of Souther Fell may be chosen from: mass hallucination or an over-indulgence in good Midsummer cheer (which amount, roughly to the same thing), or a local conspiracy which could be categorised with Hutchinson's "tales with which travellers are amused".

The floating island of Derwentwater was, and is, as real as Lodore opposite which it lies. Jonathan Otley investigated it, and sent samples of it to Dr John Dalton in 1814 for analysis; John Postlethwaite, the Lakes geologist, stood on it, and his parents had a picnic on it; and several scientific gentlemen have written detailed scientific accounts of it. A few years ago some Keswick Girl Guides planted the Union Jack on it, and claimed it for England.

The floating island has been reported as having sunk to a permanent rest; it has been measured and found to be dwindling in size, just as it has also been measured and found

Wasdale Head Church and, through the yew trees, the hotel that
was started by Auld Will Ritson

Wasdale Head and Scawfell Pike (from a nineteenth-century
drawing by Thomas Allom)

Jonathan Otley

Jonathan Otley's Mark
at the foot of Friar's
Crag is water-worn now,
but later marks record
new low-water levels

to be growing. At the start of this century Postlethwaite forecast that in a few years the island would sink forever. But it survives. It still makes its occasional appearances in the bay beside Lodore whenever there is a long spell of fine, warm weather in the late summer. That the Lake Country does not have regular, long spells of warm weather is the reason why the floating island does not surface regularly, in some seasons not at all.

For a long time the floating island was a mystery to the locals as well as to visitors: a sort of inanimate Loch Ness Monster, which was believed in by those who had seen it, scoffed at by those who had not.

It is not very spectacular, and, therefore, cannot be much of a tourist attraction, even if its appearances could be regulated. But it has given this corner of the Lake District some useful publicity, and it is not so long since its appearances were faithfully recorded alongside shipwrecks and pit disasters in the local and national newspapers.

Some said that the island did not float at all, but that it was only a section of the bed of the lake which was exposed when Derwentwater sank to abnormally low levels. Another suggestion was that it was a mass of decaying vegetable matter which floated in this corner of the lake as on the surface of a whirlpool.

Hutchinson made it clear that the floating island was talked about in his time, but he did not see it, and therefore did not believe in it.

The earliest complete account of it was put on record by the scientist-cum-clockmaker, Jonathan Otley, who examined it very thoroughly, took samples of it, drew from it some of its gaseous content, and submitted them to John Dalton for analysis. In his *Concise Description of the English Lakes* Otley says:

> It generally rises after an interval of a few years, and after a continuance of warm weather . . . It has sometimes contained about half an acre of ground, at other times only a few perches . . . Several large rents or cracks may be seen in the earth about the place, which appear to have been occasioned by its stretching to reach the surface. It never rises far above the level of the lake; but having once attained the surface, it, for a time, fluctuates with the rise and fall of

the water; after which it sinks gradually.

For a few inches in depth it is composed of a clayey or earthy matter, apparently deposited by the water, in which growing plants have fixed their roots; the rest is a congeries of decayed vegetable matter forming a stratum of loose peat earth about six feet in thickness; which rises from a bed of very fine soft clay.

Otley found "a considerable quantity of air" in the body of the island which Dr Dalton found to consist of equal parts of carburetted hydrogen (methane, or marsh gas) and azotic gasses (nitrogen), with a little carbonic acid (carbon dioxide.)

Otley plotted the appearances of the island for more than thirty years, and regarded it as extraordinary that it should appear in three successive years — 1824-5-6. In the thirty years the island appeared eleven times, and that has, roughly, been its performance rate ever since.

Some theorists supposed that it was water from a stream coming underground into the lake that caused the island to float; others supposed it was air from some irruption from the bed of the lake. But Otley was definite on this point.

The air to which the rising of this island has been attributed, is not collected in a body underneath it; but is interspersed through the whole mass.

And the most probable conclusion seems to be, that air or gas is generated in the body of the island by decomposition of the vegetable matter of which it is formed; and this gas being produced most copiously, as well as being more rarefied in hot weather, the earth at length becomes so distended therewith, as to render the mass of less weight than an equal bulk of water. The water then insinuating itself between the substratum of clay and the peat earth forming the island, bears it to the surface.

At a later date the island was examined by Dr Hugh R. Mill, who, in 1895 published *A Bathymetrical survey of the English Lakes*, and in 1888 G.J. Symons published the result of investigations he had made in an elaborate monograph entitled *The Floating Island in Derwentwater, its History and Mystery with notes on other Dissimilar Islands*. In the meantime, before either of these learned gentlemen had ventured near the floating island, John Postlethwaite had carried out his own investigations, and his were as thorough as those of Jonathan Otley, and came to roughly the same conclusions.

In 1857 Postlethwaite rowed a boat round the island, carefully examining every feature of it. Then, greatly daring, he placed one of the floorboards of the boat in the island, and stood on it, "ascertaining thereby that it was only depressed very slightly by my weight".

He was not the first to land on the island; he was literally following in his father's footsteps because a few days previously his parents had sailed over to the floating island from Brandlehow, where they lived, with provisions, a kettle and a spirit lamp, and enjoyed what surely must have been the first picnic ever held on the floating island.

Postlethwaite agreed with Otley that the floating island was not a mass of rotting vegetable matter, but a portion of the bed of the lake which was raised to the surface of the water, like a huge bubble, or, to be more exact, like a huge blister since the space beneath was filled with water and not — as had been generally supposed, despite the findings of Jonathan Otley — with gas.

In 1857 the surface of the island exposed above the lake surface measured only 10 yards by 3, and the depth of water beneath it was 3 or 4 feet.

On one side of the island Postlethwaite found rents or cracks like those described by Otley, and through one of these he pushed an oar to prove that it was all water underneath. These fissures enabled him to see that in section the floating mass consisted of from 6 to 7 inches of water-borne sediment mixed with decaying vegetable matter and interlaced with the roots of Aquatic plants. The remainder of the mass of the island, about 3 or 4 feet thick, was of black peat which also contained the roots of aquatic plants.

Whenever he pushed his stick into the matter which comprised the floating island, Postlethwaite liberated masses of bubbles which he identified as marsh gas.

Following Otley's lead, Postlethwaite argued that in hot seasons the generation of gas from the decaying vegetable matter was accellerated by the heat, and the bed of the lake was thus borne to the surface where it remained until the weather cooled and the gas either ceased to be generated, or escaped, whereupon the island sank back to rest.

The island has never been bigger, as far as records go, than in 1815 when it measured 88 yards by 25 and remained on the surface for three weeks. Its longest stay on the surface was fourteen weeks in 1831; its shortest in 1905 when it appeared on August 12 and sank only seven days later having been, as Postlethwaite said, a pale shadow of its former self. It was this that led Postlethwaite to forecast that the island who soon sink forever, overlooking the fact that after a few appearances in which its size steadily declined, it had disappeared in 1884, but reappeared after an absence of twelve years, much to everybody's surprise.

And whenever the Lake District has a long hot summer, the floating island still turns up, and can be seen best from the 'Surprise View' on the road to Watendlath.

Viewed from close quarters the floating island is not very impressive – one visitor is reported to have said "It would look better with trees!" – but it seems deceptively solid. Walking on it is not recommended.

The question has often been asked: Why should there be only one floating island in the Lakes; why are the lakes not dotted with floating islands because the conditions in Derwentwater must occur over and over again.

The answer to this is probably that the beck which flows into Derwentwater near the floating island tends, in dry weather, to diminish in flow and disappear into the gravel which normally forms its bed, the water emerging eventually from underneath and well out into the lake, under the floating island loosening the 'island' from the bed of the lake, and allowing its natural buoyancy to bring it to the surface.

The 'bottom wind', in which Hutchinson believed while mocking the idea of an island which floated, has been given some attention in the literature of the Lakes. Pennant mentioned it saying: "The water of Derwentwater is subject to violent agitations, and often without any apparent cause, as was the case this day; the weather was calm, yet the waves ran at a great height, and the boat was violently tossed with what is called a 'bottom wind'."

Gilpin also knew about the bottom wind, and wrote: "Often when all is calm and resplendent around, as the boat is plying its steady way along the glassy lake, and boatmen will decry at a distance a violent ebullition of the water. He will see it heave and swell, forced upwards by some internal convulsion, and suffering all the agitation of a storm. But as soon as the confined air has spent its force, the agitated surface immediately subsides and dies away in lessening circles."

These descriptions of the 'bottom wind' seem to have been exaggerations — on the part of the writers or their informants in the matter — of a perfectly natural experience in the Lakes: the sudden squall which can come out of nowhere in such mountainous country on the gentlest of days.

Gilpin's account suggests a violent eruption of air from the bottom of the lake — wind from the lake-bottom, in fact — which can definitely be classed among those other "tales with which travellers are amused", and has about as much basis in fact as the claim of Auld Will Ritson of Wasdale Head that he once crossed a cur with an eagle the better to get his sheep off the fellsides.

Jonathan Otley thought little of the bottom wind. As the resident expert on all things to do with Derwentwater, he was often approached for his account of both the floating island and the bottom wind, but whilst he was prepared to talk at some length about the island, he treated tales of the bottom wind with contempt and refused to comment upon it. His attitude to these subjects is apparent in his famous guide book: he gave an entire chapter to the floating island, and not a single mention to the bottom wind.

Old Jonathan was a remarkable man, and a remarkably talented man. He won fame as the author of *A Concise Description of the English Lakes* which ran to twelve editions in his lifetime, the old man taking care that each edition and its illustrations were kept up to date. He was born in Grasmere — in Nook House, the name of which was later changed, not for the better, to 'Scroggs' — where the family can be traced back to 1575, which is as far back as the Grasmere Church records go. He was the son of a wood-seive and basket-maker, and it says something for the educational standards of the artisans of Grasmere Vale that Otley senior was a good Latin scholar, and that he encouraged his son to study Latin and mathematics.

Jonathan started his schooling in Langdale, and then went

on to 'a good school' at Ambleside. This good education notwithstanding, he was destined to follow his father's trade, and inherit the business, and he worked with him until he was 25. In that time, Jonathan also learned to work with clocks and watches, with a view to widening the scope of the family business, and, as another sideline, he also taught himself to be a skilful engraver.

In 1791 he moved to Keswick because that bustling little town held out better prospects for business than his native village, and because he wished to break away from his father's trade and concentrate on watch and clock repairing. Another reason was that he had lost the first and only love of his life to the Grasmere blacksmith. He never married. He lived at Keswick for the rest of his life, and one of the first friends he made there was Peter Crosthwaite, owner and founder of Keswick's famous museum.

A careful man with his money, Jonathan lodged first with a man called Younghusband at Brow Top, paying "handsomely", he said, for his board and lodging at a shilling a day. Too handsomely, he reckoned, for he was soon at a new lodging at Brow Top with a Mr Dawson whom he paid 4s 8d a week, rising to 5s when he had been there for five years.

Jonathan kept count of his personal cost of living, and at the end of sixty-one years' residence in Keswick, he reckoned that he had paid out a total of £1325 to his Keswick landlords and landladies. He was in five different lodgings in the sixty-one years, and at the end of his life his weekly board and lodging had gone up to 10s a week.

For a long time Jonathan was Keswick's only 'clocker', and he was kept busy attending to the watches and clocks of customers from a wide district around. He lived in a yard off the Main Street, and his workroom was always known as 'Jonathan Otley's up the Steps'. The steps are still there attached to the building occupied by Young's furniture store; his room has been incorporated into the furniture showroom.

Apart from his work, at which he was an excellent craftsman, Jonathan's abiding interests were meteorology, botany and geology and he accumulated a large library of books on these subjects. His observations on Derwentwater and the fells around, and his interest in all things scientific brought him into correspondence with Professor Dalton, the chemist and propounder of the Atomic Theory, who was born at Eaglesfield, near Cockermouth.

Another friend, correspondent, and frequent visitor to Jonathan Otley's up the Steps was the celebrated geologist, Professor Adam Sedgwick, who, born at Dent, just over the Westmorland border into Yorkshire, could also be called a local product.

Jonathan published his *Guide to the Lakes* in 1823, and illustrated it with a map, and with accurate 'skylines' of fells clearly named, from half a dozen different stations in the Lake District. The engravings were his own work. Of his illustrations, Clifton Ward was later to write: "His outlines are for the most part admirably truthful and devoid of the sensational exaggeration in which too many artists are apt to indulge," which was a tilt at the licence taken by some artists in engravings of the Lake District which were appearing at the time in large numbers.

A keen correspondent, Jonathan was always seeking knowledge from well-known scientific men who counted themselves among his friends, and so he went to great pains when anybody approached him genuinely seeking enlightenment on any subject apertaining to the Lake District. He had little time, however, for people who were simply curious, and there were many of these who climbed Jonathan's steps when the little man had achieved his local fame.

An inveterate collector of information, one item which came into his hands concerned the last eagles in Borrowdale. One of his correspondents told him that the last nest in Eagle's Crag was "robbed by W. Walker and W. Youdale in 1772 or 3, and after that they got out a bird in Wything's Crag above Stonethwaite, probably about 1874 which was the last time they were known to build."

It was Otley's paper, "Remarks on the succession of the Rocks in the District of the Lakes", published in the *Philosophical Magazine* in 1820 that first attracted the attention of geologists to the Cumbrian mountains, and Professor Sedgwick, then at Cambridge, pointed out to the Geological Society of London in 1831 how Otley had been the first to recognise that the greater part of the central region of the Lake mountains was occupied by three distinct groups of stratified rocks of a slaty texture. Otley's names for these were the Claysgate, representing the Skiddaw slates; Greenstone, representing the Volcanic Series of Borrowdale, and Greywacke, the Coniston limestone and Upper Silurian of the southern part of the Lake District. Said Clifton Ward, a professional geologist engaged in the Geological Survey of the late nineteenth century, and who founded a whole string of 'Literary and Scientific' societies in Cumberland, "This threefold classification of the rocks of the mountainous country forms the basis of all the geological work in the district."

Jonathan wrote extensively, mostly articles for scientific magazines, many of them under the pseudonym 'Anthony Loajet', which was an anagram of his name.

In a life so full of achievements, it may sound strange that Jonathan Otley's principal memorial at Keswick should be an insignificant little mark on a rock at the foot of Friar's Crag. In the course of his observations on Derwentwater, he cut a notch in the rock to mark an exceptionally low level of water in the dry summer of 1824, and it was by this notch, thereafter called 'Jonathan Otley's Mark', that he measured subsequent drought levels of the lake.

In the dry summer of 1826 the lake level was twice below the mark of 1824, and in the still drier summer of 1844 it was 4 inches below the level of 1824.

Several times since the lake level has been below the mark which Jonathan Otley cut, and since Keswick has never lacked a steady supply of men wishing to imprint their initials on the town's historical records, every new low record has been marked with yet another notch, another set of initials, another date incised into a slab of slate. It is a pity Jonathan's mark was not left on its own; it is, after all, the only one which matters.

Whenever there was a dry spell, old Jonathan was there at the foot of Friar's Crag to see how the lake level measured against his mark. He was 87 when, in April 27, 1852 Dr David Ross Lietch, of Keswick, saw him picking his way to his now-famous low water mark, an encounter recorded in

"A Reminiscence of Jonathan Otley", which was printed in pamphlet form in 1882, and sold to raise money for Crosthwaite Church.

> There was something very characteristic of the man in the scene and the situation, and I should have liked very much to have had his figure drawn, as he appeared, moving along in his well-known solitary, quiet manner, amid the scenes which he had loved, and done so much to make familiar to others during more than half a century; and buried too in one of those careful, accurate observations for which he had long been famous.
>
> The evening light; the low calm, almost silent waters of the lake — for they scarcely lapped against the crag at his feet — the rough track he was treading, and all the sights and sounds which in this valley accompany the close of day, were in harmony with the idea of the old man.
>
> The waters of life were low for him now, weak as the ripple scarcely breaking on the rock; yet they were calm and bright withal.
>
> The day with him had reached its quiet evening, and though a few infirmities made his life path, like the shore he was treading, a little rough, he brought patience as hitherto to his aid, and was only the more cautious and leisurely in his steps.

Lietch and his companion, who had been watching the old man from a boat on the lake, landed and went with him to his mark on Friar's Crag where, with a piece of slate stick and an inch rule, old Jonathan went through his careful process of measuring the lake level.

In the drought of 1853 Jonathan went again to Friar's Crag to see how the depth of the lake was reduced, and the last time he was there was in the September of that year.

"I then began to feel that the old stone stairs that I had clomb for fifty-five years were too hard for me," he wrote to a friend when he finally found that 'Jonathan Otley's up the Steps' was getting out of his reach. He took a small cottage, and on leaving his old quarters he had to sell off the greater part of his books, botanical and geological specimens, and his watchmaker's tools. They went under the auctioneer's hammer. "Such a variety," wrote old Jonathan, "never was exposed in Keswick, when 336 lots were disposed of, leaving me, after expenses, about twenty pounds."

On December 7, 1856, Jonathan Otley died. He was 91.

11

The Man
Who Loved Herdwicks

a bit of meteorological and climatic survey of a quite exceptional
district going about on four legs.

Gatesgarth — there is a magic in the name. To thousands it is
evocative of climbing days in Birkness Comb, or the start or
finish of ridge walks round Nicholas Size's 'Secret Valley', of
welcome and liberal refreshment after clattering into
Warnscale Bottom from the Gables, or down Honister or
Scarth Gap.[1]

It is difficult to say what it is that makes Gatesgarth
unique. The rock climbing on the fells around is not
exceptional, the ridge walks no more spectacular than dozens
of others in the Lake District. But what wanderer of the fells
does not have a special affection for it; how many thousands
of Lakeland enthusiasts known every winding footpath on
the fellsides around as they know the lines of their own
hands?

Gatesgarth is a farm, a place of call; a place to stop for a
snack and for a 'crack'. It is one of those places where it
seems right to stop for a while whether the journey is on foot
through the fells, or by car 'doing' the Lakes in a few hours.
It is a place, hallowed for many by memories of the Nelsons
who won equal renown as farmers and as hosts, and whose
traditions are carried on by the Richardsons who own
Gatesgarth today. At clipping time at this headquarters of an
extensive stretch of Herdwick country an audience of
interested visitors is customary, and it always seems to have
been so since the Nelsons moved in here 120 years ago.

The impression is often given that the dalesmen farmers
of the Lake Country, successors to the 'statesmen' or
'estatesmen', are, like the oak trees, rooted to the land by
family for centuries. This is so in some districts, but in these
parts it is not; the dalesmen seem to have been quite mobile

from farm to farm, from valley to valley.

And so it was with the Nelsons of Gatesgarth. Even the famous Ned Nelson of Gatesgarth, was not a native of the valley. The family seem to have come from the Caldbeck area. At any rate George Nelson and his wife Ann went to Chapel Farm, Borrowdale from there. They had four sons and four daughters, Ned, or Edward, to give him his full name, being the third son.

George had a run of bad luck in Borrowdale, and to try and change it, moved to Gatesgarth. His luck did not change, so he went over into Patterdale to manage a farm for Squire Marshall, of Patterdale Hall.

Young Ned Nelson was passionately fond of sheep and he was only 10 years of age when he was given the job of looking after the hoggets when they were wintering down the valley at Loweswater.

When he was 12 years old he was hired to John Hird of Keskadale in Newlands, and then he went to work for Miss Skelton, of Foulsyke, Loweswater. He was there for eight years and during that time met and married Eleanor Banks, daughter of John Banks, the Kirkstile innkeeper. At the time of his wedding, Ned was 21, and it seemed that the Herdwicks of the fells had seen the last of him because he then settled down with his wife to run the Kirkstile.

However, Herdwicks were already too much a part of his life for him to give them up altogether, and, conveniently for him, the Kirkstile had facilities enough for him to keep a flock.

His Herdwick flock he ran more as a hobby than as a means of making a living, so he concentrated on quality; on improving the breed, and he succeeded to such an extent that when he had been at the Kirkstile fourteen years he decided to go in for sheep farming as a full-time occupation.

It happened that in 1850 the tenancy of Gatesgarth became vacant so Ned, his wife and family, and two hundred gimmers, the pick of his Kirkstile flock, moved in.

With the Gatesgarth farm went a flock of 1447 heaf-going Herdwicks, the understanding being that an outgoing tenant would leave as many sheep on the heafs as he had found there. Those two hundred gimmers raised at Loweswater, made Ned Nelson's first year at Gatesgarth quite hectic, for at every opportunity they headed westwards for their native heaf, the homing instinct being especially strong in the Herdwick breed. Ned was to recall later that it took a few generations to breed the Loweswater end of the valley out of the memories of his best Herdwicks.

Ned started showing his sheep as soon as he settled into the Kirkstile, and his first prize ticket was won in Egremont in 1836. He carried on showing for the rest of his life, and never ceased in his efforts to improve the Herdwick breed. He turned the Gatesgarth stock into the finest in the country, and out of the steepest and most rugged land in the Lakes he made a farm which was a model for all fell farmers.

His operations at 'Gasket', as they called Gatesgarth, startled the locals. He hired Irishmen to work on the drainage of the flat lands at Warnscale Bottom. Until then the beck which ran out of the Bottom was aptly named 'Crookabeck', but by the time Ned's Irishmen had finished their work it ran straight as an arrow into Buttermere.

The farm extended over 160 acres of 'inside' land on the valley bottom; the sheep heafs stretched from Scale Force over Red Pike, High Stile, High Crag, Scarth Gap and Haystacks all the way to 'Three-nooked Brandreth' on one side and covered Fleetwith, Yew Crags and the Honister fellsides on the other. His sheep-run was 8 miles long and 4 broad, and on it he ran four distinct stocks of Herdwicks: the Gatesgarth Side, and the Birkness, Scale Force and Fleetworth (Fleetwith) stocks.

Ned had a constant reminder that he was not absolute monarch of all he surveyed in the earmarks of three of his four Herdwick stocks. The Gatescarth Side, the Birkness and Scale Force stocks were all cropped on both ears, which meant that the ends of the ears were missing. This was a mark conceded only to lords of the manor, since such a privilege could only be granted to those who could be trusted − in days when sheep stealing was prevalent − with a mark which took off the greater part of both ears thus obliterating any former mark which may have been made. It was a reminder to Ned that whatever he made of Gatesgarth and its flocks, the land, the buildings and 1447 of the sheep belonged to 'Squire' Marshall, of Patterdale Hall, who was Ned's landlord.

The knowledge did not inhibit him in his work. He expanded his flocks, and he fenced in and cleared of bracken 600 acres of fellside 'intak'. In the process he became a 'character' known to thousands far outside the bounds of his native county. Sometimes he seemed cast from the same mould as his friend and contemporary Auld Will Ritson, of Wasdale Head, addicted to telling tall stories, though never so outrageously tall as those credited to the Wasdale innkeeper. He became a legend in his lifetime because of his farming activities and his work for the Herdwick breed, and his house acquired a reputation for hospitality which was second to none in the Lake Country.

He gathered some extra fame — and a little extra money — by guiding visitors over the fells. One of these was Princess Louise Countess of Lorne, daughter of Queen Victoria. In September, 1877, Her Royal Highness was visiting the Hon. Percy Wyndham, who then lived at Isel Hall. Scheduled to spend a few days at Muncaster Castle, the residence of Lord Muncaster, the princess decided to travel the hard way.

With her husband, the Marquis of Lorne, and a train of attendants, Princess Louise arrived at Gatesgarth where they had lunch in the farm house. Because she had expressed a wish to see some Herdwicks, Ned turned some of his prize tups out into the farmyard for her inspection. Some of these tups were strangers to each other and immediately assumed battle stations, each retreating a few steps before bounding forward to meet, head-on with crashes that sounded like falling rocks and proving to the princess that all sheep were not as harmless and innocent as doves.

Princess Louise was then taken on a led pony up Honister and by Brandreth and Grey Knotts and down Styhead into Wasdale. As the party descended into Wasdale, a few Herdwicks, startled by the intrusion of this large party of people, ran on ahead and prompted Auld Will Ritson, who was among the welcoming party at the foot of the Sty to remark that he thought the Princess was "a gay canny body, for she's browt her mutton wid her".

Successes for the Gatesgarth flocks at agricultural shows continued to win more than a local fame, but it was not until 1855 that Ned ventured to put his Herdwicks in front of the judges at the Royal Show. He entered them when the show was at Carlisle, and it was the only time in a career in the show yard which lasted fifty years that he came away without a prize ticket. Fellside sheep were definitely not popular with national judges.

Ned worked on at the improvement of the breed, and nine years later, in 1864, he won the first prize at the Newcastle 'Royal' with his famous tup 'Thousand-a-year'. He also took the first prize with a 5½-pound fleece from a 5-year-old wether.

When the Royal Show returned to Carlisle in 1880, Herdwicks became the centre of a controversy which raged throughout the national agricultural Press. Writing about the Royal in *The Field*, a correspondent was severely critical of the Herdwick breeders and "their hairy and black-spotted pets" and advised them to try Cheviots instead. "Cheviots," he wrote, "look in every way specimens of the result of civilisation, while the Herdwicks in every way look like the last remnant of, we won't say barbarism, but of very ancient and primitive sheep breeding." As if intent on arousing the ire of the Herdwick men, the writer went on: "The judges at Carlisle gave the prizes to sheep that had the least hair around their necks, and the fewest black spots about the back and sides . . . in the older rams the prizes went to goaty looking animals that had long black or brown ruffs of hair around their necks and long grey beards."

What Ned Nelson and his Herdwick-breeding cronies had to say about these comments when reprinted in the local newspapers is not on record, but the fell sheep found a friend and ally in a writer for the *Agricultural Gazette* who said: "If in fleece and flesh the Herdwick contributes satisfactorily to the comfort of the human residents in their own territory, why should outsiders endeavour to ridicule their breeders because Herdwicks are not Cheviots? As well might one inveigh against the flocks which graze the hills in the neighbourhood of the Tweed because they are Cheviots and not Cotswolds or Lincolns." He defended the hardiness of the Herdwicks, saying: "It is the wet, the herbage, the steepness, the exposure to wind and rain on the range held by the Herdwicks more than the mere cold which has developed their pecularities of form and covering."

He had thought the very opposite to *The Field* reporter when he looked — at Kilburn and at Carlisle — upon "the curious half-chamois looking creatures called Herdwicks." "Half-chamois" he called them; "goaty-looking" they had been described by *The Field*, and the *Gazette* writer obviously had some doubts, or was referring to the very uniqueness of the Herdwick breed when he added: "These will puzzle the angelic host to determine on the Judgment Day, whether they are to go to the right or to the left. I thought as I looked at the Herdwick classes, 'Here is a bit of meteorological, geological and climatic survey, of a quite exceptional district, going about on four legs[1]." It did not seem to him at all strange that the produce of an exceptionally situated locality should be itself exceptional.

Ned Nelson and the rest of the Herdwick breeders continued on their way, refusing to be budged from the standards they had set for their sheep. In their own country the Herdwicks were supreme, the sole source of income from thousands of acres which would otherwise be left occupied only by foxes and birds, periodically disturbed by disciples of John Peel, geologists, botanists, and enthusiastic tourists.

In 1883 *The Livestock Journal* sent a writer to examine the Gatesgarth farm and he reported that "miles away from the resources of civilisation, Mr Edward Nelson has managed to create for himself a name and a fame that are as wide as the world, and will last as long as the literature of agriculture exists."

There was a room at Gatesgarth which was unique in 1883 and which remained a showpiece for many decades afterwards. The walls, even the ceiling, were papered, every square inch, with prize tickets won by Gatesgarth Herdwicks. There were by now two thousand of these tickets including firsts and seconds at the Royal Shows at Kilburn, Liverpool, Manchester, Newcastle and Carlisle.

Also in Ned's trophy room, arrayed on shelves were further substantial proofs of his success as a Herdwick breeder. There were more than forty pieces of silver he had won: tea services, claret jugs, drinking cups, snuff boxes, purses, egg stands and silver candlesticks, even a pair of silver-plated shears won at a wool show by an especially good Gatesgarth fleece.

In addition Ned honoured the memory of his best sheep, mostly tups, by having their heads mounted on plaques and hung about the house. There was Gatesgarth Boggle, Tom and Beggar Lad; Thousand-a-Year which took top honours at the Royal Show at Newcastle in 1864, and was sold for thirty guineas. It did not seem a high price for such a celebrated tup, but Ned had insisted that he should have another year's use of it before it went to its new owner. Also looking down on visitors were the mounted heads of Toby and Young Thousand-a-Year, the latter a most promising tup which was killed by lightning in one of those sudden storms which can strike the Gatesgarth fells in high summer.

But if Thousand-a-Year was Gatesgarth's most famous tup, the real progenitor of the greatness which the flock reached was old Joe, named after the 1886 Grand National winner which was raised at Wigton and was toned down from a fiery youth by service in the shafts of a milk cart. Old Joe lived up to his name, and died, still monarch of the fells and heavily freighted with honours at the ripe old age of 17.

The work Ned Nelson put in at Gatesgarth was evident everywhere, and still is. He planted trees for shelter belts around the farm, and he dredged tons of gravel off the shore of Buttermere and out of the streams to lay good hard roads around the farmstead. He built a barn, 11 by 33 yards, enormous by Lakeland standards, and added a huge wool shed which never seemed big enough to hold his entire wool clip.

He measured his wealth, not only by what he had in the bank, but in the number of sheep grazing his heafs in addition to the original heaf-going flock of 1,447.

The present Gatesgarth flock, still in the same four stocks as in Nelson's time, totals about 2,500, and it is unlikely that Ned had any more than that if only because of his concentration on quality above quantity.

A description of Gatesgarth was written in 1878 by Thomas Farrall, of Aspatria. Farrall reported that the total

Derwentwater's floating island (*upper right*) from the 'Surprise View' on the road to Watendlath

Straightened by Auld Ned Nelson in his Gatescarth drainage operations, 'Crookabeck' at the head of Buttermere is reverting to its meandering course again

Herdwick rams

Shearing Herdwicks at Gatescarth, 1972

ram stock at Gatesgarth was 150, some for breeding, some for sale, and some for hiring to other Herdwick flock-masters. This hiring of tups was, and still is customary among the fells, the idea being to prevent the flocks from becoming too 'keen' bred.

Gatesgarth tups realised between £20 and £30 at sales, and those hired to other flocks were let for the season at between £12 and £18, which was very expensive.

At the end of November each year, Ned brought his ewes down from the fells into the 'inside' land and sorted them into lots of sixty or seventy. One tup was put in with each lot for Ned had discovered that the segregating of ewes into these 'harems' for his tups meant stronger lambs. In the free-for-all which had ensued when groups of rams were put into flocks of ewes, a great deal of the tups' energy was dissipated in battling for flock supremacy, the animals fighting for hours in head-to-head crashes which aroused the echoes from the fells.

Apart for saving the strength of his tups for the business in hand, Ned's method of segregating them in groups gave him a better control of his breeding lines.

At the end of three weeks each lot of ewes was given the mark of the ram they had been with, and the rams were removed and put into loose boxes. There they were fed with corn and hay until Ned considered that they were again 'fully made up'.

The tups were the spoiled darlings of the flock; at New Year the ewes were back on the fells where they remained for twenty-one weeks until lambing time when those which were most forward were brought down to the lambing garths under the eye of the shepherd. As soon as the lambs were strong enough both lambs and ewes were sent back to the fell.

There were losses of course. Foxes took up to seventy-five lambs a year which was why the Melbreak Foxhounds were always welcome there. To make up for these ewes' losses twin lambs were separated, it having long been accepted in the best Herdwick circles that one lamb was as much as any ewe could be expected to rear.

To get ewes to foster lambs a method was used which

had proved successful for centuries, and which is still in use today. If the ewe's dead lamb was available, it was skinned and the skin tied to the back of a live one. Then both ewe and lamb were consigned to a dark room for twelve hours after which there usually seemed to be a pretty good understanding between the two.

Lambs were dipped at shearing time, and six weeks later the entire flock was brought down and dipped against blow-fly, and a thorough dipping at Martinmas finished the programme for the year.

For the tups, the flower of the flock, there was special treatment. In addition to the dipping, they were also salved — a messy business, but considered necessary for such valuable animals. The salve consisted of a mixture of rancid butter, or any other available grease, and tar, and the operation consisted of taking a handful of this evil-smelling mixture and rubbing it deep into the fleeces.

This was the old method of repelling sheep pests, used on entire flocks before dipping was introduced. The repellant effect of the salve was obvious to the nostrils of human beings and kept non-sheep breeding people from social contact with the Herdwick folk at salving time. Everybody detested salving sheep because, unlike other communal tasks like harvest or sheep-clipping, few ever had any inclination to round off a day's salving with anything but a good wash, a change of clothes, and a fervent hope that the salve would not flavour the supper.

For different flocks there were different salves, all depending upon what sort of fat or grease was available as the 'spreader'. Each salve, therefore, had a different smell, which led a visiting cleric to coin one of the more colourful Lakeland-derived descriptions for particularly noissome occasions: "A congregation of smells, like Wasdale Head Church at sheep salving time."

For their first winter the hoggets — the first year females — were sent to pasture in coastal farmlands at a cost of half a crown a head to lead a celibate first winter with a view of building them up for their subsequent life of lamb bearing on the meagre forage of their native heafs.

In the hardest of winters the Gatesgarth ewes had to

fend for themselves without even a handful of hay to help them out when the fells were covered with frozen snow. It was the sort of life they had been bred to lead, and it was obviously the sort of life they preferred.

Herdwick mutton is not among the gourmet foods today, and it was not greatly thought of in the past, except by the Herdwick men themselves. Ned Nelson, however, had a special market for his wethers, or castrated rams. "At four years," wrote Thomas Farrall, "the flesh of the Herdwick wether is calculated to serve the taste of the most fastidious epicure, being ripe, juicy and unsurpassingly sweet."

On the subject of wethers, the following tale is told of Ned Nelson. He bred, or bought, a tup of which great things were expected. Its performance, however, did not come up to its promise. One bright November day Ned was out at the pen contemplating this failure of a tup and its unserved harem of ewes when a friend came along and hailed him: "Morning, Ned. Fine weather!"

"Nay," replied Ned, sourly, "but it will be tomorrow."

He travelled all over the northern two-thirds of England showing his Herdwicks, and did more for the breed than anybody before or since. As far as he was concerned there was no other breed of sheep worth bothering about at the place he had chosen for his life's labour, and he showed a concern for his sheep which was a model for other men showing sheep at agricultural meetings.

When he had them at a show, he seldom let them out of his sight, and once, when the Royal Show was at Liverpool, he met an acquaintance who asked him where he was staying. "Oh," said Ned, "I'm stopping in 'Ardwick Street'", which must have sounded all right to his questioner, but which actually meant that he was sleeping in the alley beside the Herdwick pens.

Apart from the sheep, Ned grazed about thirty cattle at Gatesgarth. He had most of the fences erected, but the stone walls which zig-zagged over the fellsides were there long before he arrived. He saw that the walls were kept in good repair, a mammoth task considering that he had the care of some 20 miles of them. Asked how often he covered the bounds of his farm, he would say "As often as Ah hev to". Sometimes he went on foot, sometimes on a sturdy fell pony, often with a lamb or an injured ewe as passengers.

Even the cur dogs at Gatesgarth were something special. There were never less than eight working sheepdogs all of them predominantly black and all descended from an old bitch which had no less than 102 pups in her lifetime.

When he had passed 65 years of age, Ned was asked when he was going to retire, and he replied: "When I can take no more."

In 1885 he had his last Royal Show success at Preston, and the same year he whittled down his flocks by holding a great sale which brought in breeders from all over the Lakes.

On the last Monday in March, 1887 he was at Cockermouth market meeting his old friends, and a week later he was dead. He had lived a very full life and had made innumerable friends. He had laid in a store of experience which he was always willing to put at the disposal of younger friends either on matters of fell lore, or the raising of Herdwicks.

He had only one great disappointment. He regretted that he had no written proof that H.R.H. the Princess Louise and her husband, the Marquis of Lorne, had had lunch at Gatesgarth on the memorable occasion which had culminated in Ned guiding them over into Wasdale. As long as the Nelsons had welcomed visitors to their house and farm, a visitors' book had been kept on a table in the trophy room. Ned's Royal visitor and her husband, like everybody else, went to inspect the trophies, but for once in his life Ned was overcome by the importance of the occasion and forgot to ask them to sign his book.

12

Ghosts, Rank Upon Rank

The 'foolish fire' on Souther Fell

It is possible among the Lake District mountains, and under the right conditions, to see a Brocken-type 'spectre'.* The sun must be low in the sky, and the observer on a mountain top with a cloud or mist conveniently behind. Then the observer's shadow will be cast upon the cloud ... and that is the 'spectre'. Such 'spectres' have been seen so often that they no longer merit a mention in the local newspapers.

In an area where superstition was rife, it was natural that ghost stories would be generated; among an unsophisticated people it was natural that some of them would be believed. That ghost stories could survive to be handed down from generation to generation and finally passed on to what the local people considered to be a gullible flock of visitors is equally natural.

Within living memory, it was a popular pastime among Cumbrians to sit around the fire at nights and talk. It has now gone out of fashion, and television and the radio have taken over. In the limited world in which they lived, subjects for conversation were often sparse, and then the natural inventiveness of the Cumbrian took over, and the ghost story was the result.

Some of the ghost stories were purely for domestic consumption like the Cass How Boggle near Lorton, and the Salterbeck and Branthwaite Neuk boggles in West Cumberland, all of which had their origins in memories of

* The Brocken is the highest summit in the Hartz mountains in Germany. It is celebrated for the Brockengespeust or 'spectre of the Brocken' which is the shadow of men thrown upon low cloud or mist by the setting sun.

violence: suicide in the case of the Cass How Boggle, and murder in the other two.

The use of the word 'boggle' seems to signify that these ghosts were strictly for local consumption. More distinguished apparitions had much more dramatic titles, like The Skulls of Calgarth, the Crier of Claife, and the Ghost Army of Souther Fell.

The Skulls of Calgarth and the Crier of Claife were distinctly on the tourist route through the Lake Country and had distinguished settings, the one in Calgarth Hall, the other at the Windermere ferry where the Crier, with an abode on Claife Heights, cried like the Sirens to lure ferrymen and their passengers to death. The Crier of Claife was of ancient origin and posterity could not be blamed for thinking that it had a hand in the ferry accident of 1635 in which forty-seven people were drowned, an event commemmorated in "The Fatall Nuptiall" by Richard Brathwaite.[1]

It has even been suggested that this tragedy gave birth to the legend of the Crier of Claife, but Brathwaite must already have been aware of the story because he is at pains to deny that the accident was caused by

> Some hideous Hagge, or late-deprived Witch
> Sprung from those desert Concaves, forlorne Cells,
> Raising these stormes with their infernall Spells.

Whatever mischief the Crier of Claife is alleged to have commited, and there have been other ferry accidents; there is no danger today for, apart from the ferry being a robust and reliable affair, the Crier was exorcised by a priest specially brought in for the job, according to tradition.

The truly classic ghost story of the Lake Country is that of the Ghost Army of Souther Fell (pronounced Souter, sometimes Sutor, both of which are old spellings of the name) which appears in Hutchinson's *History of Cumberland*. It is quoted from 'Mr Smith', who is none other than the intrepid 'G.S.', whose expedition to the wedd mines of Borrowdale and the country beyond seemed such a death-defying affair. It appears in an article which Smith wrote about a journey over Caldbeck, Saddleback and Souther fells with, as Hutchinson puts it so succinctly "an account of a remarkable Ingnis Fatuus."

Smith, not averse to creating a wrong impression among readers who were unlikely to check on his findings, was on form: the form he was to use on his descriptions of his visit to the wadd mines, and, in the neighbourhood of Mosedale found "villages in the narrow bottoms that feel no more benefit from the solar rays, for two months, about the winter solstice, than the old Cimmerians, or the Laplanders who inhabit the North cape of Norway".

He writes of the mountain ash — "very beautiful when the fruit is ripe" — and adds: "the superstitious use it against witchcraft", which was true at the time because farm wives used a stick of it to stir cream and ensure that the cream turned to butter.

Smith saw Bowscale Tarn the singularity of which was that "several of the most credible inhabitants thereabouts affirm that they frequently see the stars in it at mid-day", a phenomenon which required conditions which did not exist during his visit — a familiar excuse given by retailers of folklore to the credulous visitor, like the immortal trout in the same tarn which prove their immorality by never being caught.

But to Souther Fell:

"a distinguished mountain of itself [where] the astonishing phenomenon appeared to exhibit itself, which, in 1735, 1737, and 1745, made so much noise in the north, that I went on purpose to examine the spectators, who asserted the fact, and continue in their assertion very positively to this day.

On Midsummer eve, 1735, William Lancaster's servant related that he saw the east side of Souter-fell, towards the top, covered with a regular marching army for above an hour together; he said they consisted of distinct bodies of troops, which appeared to proceed from an eminence in the north end, and marched over a niche in the top, (marked A and B in the place) [a map which is reproduced by Hutchinson and which stretches credibility even further than the story of the ghost army] but, as no other person in the neighbourhood had seen the like, he was discredited and laughed at.

Two years after, on Midsummer eve also, betwixt the hours of eight and nine, William Lancaster himself imagined that several gentlemen were following their horses at a distance, as if they had been hunting, and taking them for such, he paid no regard to it, till about ten minutes after, again turning his head towards the place, they appeared to be mounted, and a vast army following, five in rank, crowding over at the same place where the servant said he saw them two years before. He then called his family, who all agreed in the same opinion; and, what was most extraordinary, he frequently observed that some one of the five would quit rank, and seem to stand in a fronting posture, as if he was observing and regulating the order of their march, or taking account of their numbers, and, after some time, appeared to return full gallop to the station he had left, which they never failed to do as often as they quitted their lines; and the figure that did so was generally one of the middlemost men in the rank. As it grew later, they seemed more regardless of discipline, and rather had the appearance of people riding from a market, than an army; though they continued crowding on, and marching off, so long as they had light to see them.

This phenomenon was no more seen till the Midsummer eve which preceded the rebellion, when they were determined to call more families to be witness of this sight, and accordingly went to Wilton-hill and Souter-fell side, till they convened about 26 persons, who all affirm they then saw the same appearance, but not conducted with the usual regularity as the preceding ones, having the likeness of carriages interspersed; however, it did not appear less real; for some of the company were so affected with it, as, in the morning, to climb the mountain, through an idle expectation of finding horse shoes after so numerous an army; but saw not the vestige or print of a foot.

William Lancaster, indeed, told me that he never concluded they were real beings, because of the impracticability of a march over the precipices where they seemed to come on; that the night was extremely serene; that horse and man, upon strict looking at, appeared to be but one being, rather than two distinct ones; that they were nothing like any clouds or vapours which he had ever perceived elsewhere; that their number was incredible, for they filled lengthways near half a mile, and continued so in a swift march for above an hour, and much longer, he thinks, if night had kept off.

The last phrase is important in William Lancaster's story told to George Smith because this 'ghost' went contrary to most ghostly visitations by appearing in broad daylight mostly, and ending only when darkness descended. Smith went on:

The whole story has so much the air of romance, that it seemed fitter for 'Amedis de Gaul' or 'Glenville's System of Witches', than the repository of the learned; but as the country was full of it, I only give it verbatim from the original relation of a people that could have no end in imposing on their fellow creatures, and are of good repute in the place where they live.

It is my real opinion that they apprehended they saw such appearances; but how an undulating lambient meteor could affect the optics of many people is difficult to say. No doubt fancy will extend to miraculous heights in persons disposed to indulge it; and whether there might not be a concurrence of that to assist the vapour, I will not dispute, because three difficulties seem to occur worthy of solution.

Smith had made up his mind on one point, and that was that the "appearance" was an "undulating lambent meteor". This still left the solution wide open for any atmospheric phenomenon was called a 'meteor', and his use of the adjective "Lambent" ("of flame or light — playing on the surface without burning it," *Oxford English Dictionary*), and "undulating" to describe the movement, firmly (if that word can be used in the context of this tale at all) puts the whole thing into the category which Hutchinson originally chose for it: 'Ignis-Fatuus', or Will o' the Wisp, or, literally, 'foolish fire'.

But Smith still had his three "difficulties"; his three unanswered questions. The first was why a lambent agitated meteor should appear to stop at certain intervals, and return with augmented velocity to re-assume the forsaken place. He was referring to Lancaster's account of the middle members of ranks quitting and then returning to the ranks.

The second was why it should, for a very long time, preserve so regular a system and appear in ranks of five.

The third was why the appearance should occur on one particular evening of the year, three times at such long intervals. "These are at present beyond my philosophy to explain," wrote Smith. "Those who treat it as a mere illusion should assign reasons for so large a fascination in above 20 persons; probably one, indeed, might serve to aggrandise the fancy of others; but I should think they could not be so universally deceived without some stamina of the likeness exhibited on the mountain from a meteor or from some unknown cause."

Smith's account of the ghost army was written within four years after its last appearance, before his death-defying trip to Seathwaite and the wadd mines which he had had to delay "as they are kept close up, and the weather was extremely unfavourable". Instead he went on the walk over Caldbeck, Saddleback and Souther Fells. He finally made his journey to the wadd mines in 1749.

It was forty years after the army's last march that Clarke came along, and added little to the original account except to give the name of Mr Lancaster's servant, who first observed the phenomenon, as Daniel Stricket, whom Clark found living under Skiddaw and had come on in the world to the extent that he was now an auctioneer, which, the cynic might say, was a happy choice of career for a man who could sell a ghost army to an entire community.

Clarke also mentioned that it was from Blakehills, on the other side of the Glenderamakin beck from Souther Fell, that the last appearance was seen, and that the vision lasted two hours and a half, which was an advance on the "above an hour" which Lancaster had recorded.

But Clarke obtained from those who said they had seen the ghost army an attestation stating: "We, whose names are hereunto subscribed, declare the above account to be true, and that we saw the phaenomenon as here related. As witness our hands, this 21st day of July, 1785."

The date of this declaration suggests that Clarke had probably been in the district on Midsummer Day that year in the hope of seeing the ghost army for himself, and, not having seen it – probably having expressed some doubt about it – goaded the local inhabitants into making and signing their attestation.

People have been known, in recent years, to spend some time on or within sight of the rather blank face of Souther Fell in the hope of seeing yet another visit by the ghost army. There is a signpost on the A66 near to the White Horse Inn at Threlkeld which points the way to Souther Fell as if implying it has some special significance in comparison with the innumerable Lake District fells which are not so signposted. Nobody has seen anything since that historic day in 1745.

13

The Vale of St John and Poet John

Oor real wants ur nobbut few,
If we to limit them wad try.

The becks which fall from the fellsides into the river Grata whose lively water brightens the Keswick scene have names which roll splendidly off the tongue; names which are in themselves memories of the times when the Celts held away in the district. Glenderamakin Beck which flows out from behind haunted Souther Fell by way of Mungrisdale; the Glendersterra Beck which drains that part of the Skiddaw range between Lonscale Fell and Blease Fell; Naddle Beck, a name evocative of tumbling water; Blencathra, recalling wild and magic times. By contrast with these names, St John's Beck seems mild, controlled and civilised.

Mild and controlled it certainly is because St John's Beck starts off as the compensation water Manchester Corporation, probably reluctantly, allows past the Thirlmere dam. Its civilised surroundings, and certainly its name came from date from the days when the Knights Hospitaller of St John, those pioneers of the art of doing good, founded a 'hospital' or hostel on the saddle of the pass between Naddle and what is now the Vale of St John.

The civilising influence of a St John's hostel was probably needed in this wild part of Lakeland; its shelter would be welcome to travellers on a road which today seems to be at the back of beyond, but which in the thirteenth century was probably a principal traffic route. Today this seems a strange route for traffic to take, but so do so many of the other routes along which trade goods were carried. The choice of this route over the wild fell, and the siting of a hostel there was probably dictated by the conditions in an area in which all the natives were probably not hostile, but a proportion of whom could be grouped under the general description of 'lawless'.

If 'desperate banditti' in the Forest of Inglewood caused Ranulph Engain, the chief forester, to grant a licence to the prior of Carlisle to build a hospital at Caldbeck for the express purpose of relieving unfortunate travellers, there is no reason to suppose that the activities of the 'banditti' did not extend to other parts of the neighbourhood where easy pickings were available from travellers and pack trains.[1]

And so the Knights Hospitaller founded their hostel which would turn, in the natural course of development over the centuries, into an inn, although the Knights Hospitaller took their religion seriously enough to ensure that where they set up a hostel to cater for the bodily needs of the wayfarer, they also dedicated a chapel for his spiritual needs.

Inn and chapel in close proximity gave rise to Defoe's well-known quatrain:

> Wherever God erects a house of prayer,
> The Devil always builds a church there;
> And 'twill be found upon examination
> The latter has the largest congregation.

However, in contradiction to Defoe, the house of prayer came second at St John's.

The school followed in due course, and so there was established on this bleak spot the classic parish group of school, inn and chapel, the chapel building doubling as the school during the week as the reader of the little dale chapel also doubled as schoolmaster. Yet another parish amenity was introduced on the edge of this little group, higher up the fellside. This was the parish cockpit.

This, then, was the hub of the activities of a wide, wild mountain area. The chapel of St John eventually became a chapel of St Kentigern's Church, Crosthwaite, and its reader was paid £4 17s 6d a year in 1717 when Bishop Nicolson wrote: "As mean as these salaries look, the readers in these dales are commonly more rich than the curates in other parts of the diocese; having the Advantage of Drawing Bills, Bonds, Conveyances, Wills etc., which the attornies elsewhere claim as their property." The chapel gave its name to the Vale of St John, later to the Castle Rock of St John which the dalesmen of old were content to call Green Crag.

That was before some early visitor decided that Green Crag had the appearance of a castle; before Hutchinson invested it with an almost magical quality; centuries before Sir Walter Scott, no doubt influenced by Hutchinson, wove the Castle Rock into his Bridal of Triermain, and gave the excuse for yet another name: 'The Castle Rock of Triermain.'

Pennant said of the Vale of St John: "Travellers have a strange and horrible view downwards into a deep and misty vale, at this time appearing bottomless, and winding far amidst the mountains, darkened by their heights and by the thick clouds that lay on their summits."

In his *History and Antiquities of Cumberland*, 1794 Hutchinson says: "In the widest part of the vale you are struck with the appearance of an ancient ruined castle which rises from the summit of a little mount; the mountains around forming an august amphitheatre. These massive bulwarks shew a front apparently of various towers, making an awful, rude, and Gothic figure with their shaken walls and rugged battlements," and then he goes on to dispel the image by adding: "this whole figure of a powerful fortress is no other than a separate broken and ragged rock called Green Crag which stands threatening the valley."

In his *Excursion to the Lakes in Westmoreland and Cumberland*, twenty years earlier, Hutchinson had allowed his imagination to run riot.

The traveller's curiosity is roused, and he prepares to make a nearer approach; when his curiosity is put upon the rack by being assured that if he advances certain genii, who govern the place, by virtue of their superior arts and necromancy, will strip it of all its beauties and by inchantment transform its magic walls.

"The vale seems adapted for the habitation of such beings — there was no delusion in this report, we were soon convinced of its truth — for this piece of antiquity, so venerable and noble in its aspect, as we drew near changed its figure, and proved no other than a shaken massive pile of rocks which stand in the midst of this little vale, disunited from the adjoining mountains, and have so much the real form and semblance of a castle, that they bear the name of The Castle Rock of St. John's.

Avidly seeking material for his tremendous output, Sir
Walter Scott seized upon the Castle Rock and borrowed
part of the Hutchinson magic formula for his "Bridal of
Triermain". Spirited away by Merlin from the tournament
at Carlisle in which the knights of King Arthur fought so
earnestly for her hand that the Round Table was in danger
of extermination, the beautiful Gyneth was put to sleep in
the enchanted castle. There she slept for five hundred years
until Sir Roland de Vaux, Baron of Triermain, rode forth
to break the magic spell. Hutchinson's "certain genii' could
turn the castle into the rock at will, but Scott reversed the
process, and Sir Roland's axe, hurled at the rock, dissolved
the spell and:

> down the headlong ruin came,
> With cloud of dust and flash of flame.
> "When ceased the thunder, Triermain
> Surveyed the mound's rough front again;
> And lo! the ruin had laid bare,
> Hewn in stone a winding stair,
> Whose moss'd and fractured steps might lend
> The means the summit to ascend,
> And by whose aid the brave de Vaux
> Began to scale those magic rocks,
> And soon a platform won,
> Where the wild witchery to close,
> Within three lances' length arose
> The Castle of St. John.

Today the magic spell is inoperative, and no matter what
the conditions the Castle Rock looks like a rock. No
climber has ever felt impelled to hurl an ice axe at it in
emulation of Sir Roland de Vaux to reveal a magic staircase
because climbers prefer to do it the hard way.

Perhaps it was the folklore and the fictions surrounding
the Rock that kept climbers away from it until the 1930s
when the newspapers trumpeted the news that the Castle
Rock of Triermain had been conquered. The 'conquest'
loses some of the glory because, like almost all the classic
climbing scenes in the Lake Country, there is an easy way
up the back. Nowadays the Castle Rock is regularly decor-
ated with strings of striving climbers heading for the top;
but from no point, except perhaps from the bottom, roped

up and ready to go, is it as impressive as Hutchinson made it seem. Perhaps the forest of foreign conifers planted around its base have removed the magic.

There are changes, too, at the traditional site of the hospice. The inn has disappeared, its site swallowed up in a churchyard extension; the school which was eventually built is now the Diocesan Youth Centre, a headquarters for holidaying young people. Even the church is changed, for it was rebuilt in 1845.

No church in the diocese has a more dramatic setting; more spectacular surroundings. No 'modern' — and modern in this context means any time after they started building or rebuilding churches in thanksgiving for winning the Napoleonic Wars — church in the county holds better the shape and the spirit of the church which it replaced.

Seathwaite in the Vale of Duddon was given a 'town' church to replace the 'lowly house of prayer' at which 'Wonderful' Walker presided; Loweswater was given a bigger and better St Bartholomew's on the promise — fortunately unfulfilled — of the development of a mineral mining industry.

The new church of the parish of St John's-in-the-Vale is certainly distinguishable from the usual run of Lake Country churches, but it is still plain, low and small, and has a miniature tower at the west which is not much bigger than a chimney. It is still very much a dales chapel and the secret of this preservation of a traditional shape in what was virtually a new chapel lies partly in the fact that the man who carried out the rebuilding was a dalesman himself, a native of the parish, John Richardson.

Richardson is, perhaps, the most famous son of the parish, and he achieved his fame without ever leaving the place. Born in 1817 in Stone House (later Piper House), he was expected to follow in his father's trade. The father was styled a mason, but masons usually built walls, so with the directness so typical of Cumberland dialect, he was called simply a 'waller' or, to be more exact, a 'wa'er'. He could, and did, turn his hand to anything in the building line, the country craftsmen of the time being unconcerned about who did what in any branch of their industries.

From the Ferry Nab, Windermere

The river Irt at Strands, Wasdale
The river Ehen at Wath Brow

Richardson was soon taking contracts on his own in the district. He built Derwent Place in Keswick, and other houses and rows and clusters of houses in the district, but he took the greatest care in his work in the parish for he built the little school next to the church; he built the parsonage; and the restoration of the church was left in his hands.

From the lucrative but physically demanding trade of building he turned, after twenty-five years, to teaching: to building up the characters and forming the minds of the children of the parish.

Living at Bridge House at the foot of the road which rises to the Church, he was schoolmaster for about twenty-seven years. His wife, Grace, a daughter of the house of Birkett, of City House, Wythburn, went wholeheartedly along with John in his change of career, not least because they had eight children of their own to educate.

Before he changed his career, John Richardson had laid down his blueprint for a full life and happiness in a dialect poem which he entitled "What I'd wish for", and in which he gave full sway to a youthful, rustic philosophy.

If "Providence with bounteous hand" were to grant all John's wishes, he would have no empty power or heaps of wealth,

> Bit furst I'd wish for peace of mind,
> Wi' conscience free frae owt 'at's wrang,
> An' than, whativver comes amiss,
> I cudden't be unhappy lang.

A snug cottage with a rustic porch, a bit of garden ground; "some shelves o' beuks, lang neets to cheer"; a newspaper twice a week,[2] and a beck:

> Where I, wi' fishing rod could gang
> An' flog an' watch for t' risin' troot.

He wanted "just brass enough to pay his way," a wife to love and trust, and barns (bairns) whom he would have

> Industrious, sober, free frae pride;
> Upreet, an' oppen-heartit still.

John added to his list of wishes "a friend or two 'at I could trust through clood an' shine", and ended his recipe for happiness:

> I think theer nowt I want beside —
> Bit oh! We're hard to satisfy;
> Oor real wants ur nobbut few,
> If we to limit them wad try.

This was indeed the sort of life John Richardson was to lead while he built and mended walls, and when he taught school at St John's.

He was the supreme example of one of the popular images of the Lake Country dalesmen — quiet, resolute, kind-hearted and self-effacing. The other popular image was of the lusty, loud man, not averse to boasting (especially if talking about his own Herdwicks in comparison with a neighbour's), or bursting into sudden song when well lubricated after a day's hunting on the fells.

His work, when studied, is characteristic of all that is known about the author: the product of a thoughtful mind and a sympathetic heart. He did not aim high: his quest for ideas seldom took him beyond the actual experiences of his life or the tranquil scenes in which he moved. He never followed the examples of some of the 'classic' writers of dialect in looking into the rowdy, bawdy atmosphere of 'murry nests' or village weddings for his poetry. He wrote only of the placid life he knew; the life for which he had wished when he was young, and which he knew he had achieved when he reached old age.

It has often been said that it is impossible to get anything romantic out of the Cumbrian dialect; that it is a language for fratching and fighting rather than for loving, but John Richardson achieved the impossible in what has become one of the classics of Cumberland dialect.

Like the foxes of the fells around them the men who lived in the dales made long night love journeys to meet, or often just to catch a glimpse of the girls of their choice, or on whom their hopes were pinned, and it is a tender incident at the end of such a journey that is the subject of "It's nobbut me!"

It was a long walk to City House, Wythburn, where Grace lived, from John's home in St John's Vale, and since social gatherings, at which meetings were possible and where courtships began, were few and far between, it seems that John had taken a shy sort of initiative; that is if "It's nobbut me!" is truly the story of his courtship as most who knew the pair said it was.

The poem tells the story from the girl's side:

> Ya winter neet; I mind it weel,
> Oor lads 'ed been at t' fell,
> An' bein' tir't, went seun to bed,
> An' I sat be messel.
> I hard a jike on t' window pane,
> An' deftly went to see;
> Bit when I ax't 'Who's jiken theer?'
> Says t' chap, 'It's nobbut me!'
>
> 'Who's me? says I, 'What want ye here?
> Oor fwoak ur aw abed?' —
> 'I dunnet want your fwok at aw,
> It's thee I want,' he said.
> 'What can t'e want wi' me,' says I;
> 'An' who the deuce can 't be?
> Just tell me who it is an' then' —
> Says he, 'It's nobbut me.'
>
> 'I want a sweetheart, an' I thowt
> Thoo mebby wad an' aw;
> I'd been a bit down t' deal to-neet,
> An' thowt 'at I wad caw;
> What, can t' like me dus t'e think?
> I think I wad like thee' —
> 'I dunnet know who 'tis,' says I;
> Says he, 'It's nobbut me.'
>
> We pestit on a canny while,
> I thowt his voice I kennt;
> An' than I steall quite whisht away,
> An' oot at t' dooer I went.
> I creapp, an' gat 'im be t' cwoat laps,
> 'Twas dark, he cuddent see;
> He startit roond, an' said, 'Who's that?'
> Says I, 'It's nobbut me.'
>
> An' meanny a time he come ageann,

An' menny a time I went,
An' said, 'Who's that 'at's jiken theer?'
When gaily well I kent;
An' mainly what t' seamm answer com,
Frae back o' t' laylick tree;
He sed, 'I think thoo knows who't is;
Thoo knows it's nobbut me.'

It's twenty year an' mair sen than,
An' ups an' doons we've hed;
An' six fine barns hev blest us beath,
Sen Jim an' me war wed.
An' many a time I've known 'im steal,
When I'd yan on me knee,
To mak me start, an' than wad laugh —
'Ha! Ha! It's nobbut me.' "

In all the Richardsons had ten children, but two died in
infancy. Of the rest, one gained a responsible position in a
New Zealand bank, and all the other sons had good
positions in other parts of the country. A schoolmaster's
sons did not have the links which tied the sons of
statesmen to the countryside of their birth.

All Richardson's dialect work is about his personal
experiences. His "Barrin' Oot", a story of the old Cumberland custom of barring the schoolmaster out of school until
he had met the pupils' demands for a non-statutory
holiday, and a few pennies besides — a sort of old-time
sit-in without violence — was based on an actual experience
at St John's School, and the schoolmaster was Priest
Wilson, who combined the duties of schoolmaster and
priest for the parish, and who set Richardson's course
eventually to become a teacher himself.

He seems to have started writing his poetry early in life,
but it was not until he became schoolmaster at St John's-
in-the-Vale that he gave full rein to his gift. He was 54
when his first book was published in 1871 under the title:
*Cummerland Talk; being short tales and rhymes in the
dialect of that County*. A second book followed in 1876,
both published by George Coward of Carlisle, and they
both met with success, so much so that Craig Gibson, then
recognised as the ultimate living authority on dialect
writing, bestowed unstinted praise on the schoolmaster of
St John's.

At the time, Gibson was in the process of collecting pictures for a sort of Roll of Honour of dialect writers "engaged in a group with Miss Blamire as the centre."[3]

Whether Gibson ever succeeded in collecting a complete set of portraits is not known, but since in a letter to John Richardson he suggested that it would make a fine frontispiece to George Coward's collection of *Songs and Ballads of Cumberland*, and since that book came out with a picture of Susannah Blamire alone as its frontispiece, it is likely that some of the best of the then current dialect writers preferred to blush unseen, unlike Gibson who had his portrait specially taken, of all places, in Constantinople.

John Richardson went on, teaching the children, writing his poetry. He read papers to local Literary and Scientific Societies, and for a long time contributed dialect stories to the *West Cumberland Times* entitled "Stwories Ganny Used To Tell," which were actual scenes and incidents described to him, and in the original dialect of Mrs Richardson's mother, Mrs Birkett, who died about 1870 aged over 90.

He wrote a well-known hunting song, "John Crozier's Tally-ho", about the man who was responsible for the foundation of the pack of foxhounds which eventually became the Blencathra Foxhounds, and hunted them from Threlkeld.

"John Crozier's Tally-ho" attracted the attention of William Metcalfe who set it to music, hoping to achieve with it the success he had made of "D'ye ken John Peel?" But the Caldbeck hunting song was already up and away, and no other had a hope of catching it. More successful was Metcalfe's setting of "It's nobbut me" which became a 'standard' for concerts all over the county.

His other poems included "Jemmy Stubbs' Grunstean", "Jobby Dixon", "The Cockney in Mosedale", "Coming Home Sober", "The Fell King", and "Thowts by Thirlmere."

In his successful novel *Shadow of a Crime*, Hall Caine used a collection of local proverbs which Richardson put together for him, and the dales schoolmaster was also consulted on points touching the dialect by Dr Murray, editor of the *New English Dictionary*.

John subscribed to the strongly-held Cumbrian belief

that it was more important that things should be done properly, than quickly. Time was held to be cheaper than most other things, and that was why he seldom hurried over anything.

When he was a working stone-waller he had plenty of visitors at every job to inspect the work, pass opinions, and perhaps waste some of his time, but that was the way of the people, and when it came to his turn to stand and watch; when he had taught his last lesson at the little school he had himself built beside the church among the mountains, he spent a great deal of his time there.

In his old age, John Richardson took his visitors to be shown the progress being made on the wall of the new churchyard extension, delighting in passing on the knowledge that this was the first extension ever to be added to the churchyard since it was licensed for burials, prior to which all the local people were buried in the parish church of Crosthwaite.

Almost every day he spent some of his time watching the wa'er building the new wall, using new stones from the fellsides, or old stones dug out of the ruins of the old inn whose site was being incorporated into the extension. He explained to anybody who happened to be with him that when the church was first given its licence for burials, the dalesmen of St John's, who perhaps only attended two or three funerals a year at most, decided that never, as long as time lasted, would there be sufficient people dying to fill more than a rood of ground, and so that was the size they made their new churchyard.

That was some time in the early eighteenth century, and for the first twenty years of the existence of the churchyard it seemed that the dalesmen, in allocating a rood of ground, had erred on the side of generosity because the churchyard remained persistently empty. It was not that people had stopped dying in this parish with its people scattered so thinly over its fair face. There was a locally-held belief that the devil was waiting to claim the soul of the first person to be buried in the new churchyard, so the dalesmen continued to insist upon interment at Crosthwaite.

The records of St John's Church do not show who it was who first-footed into the new churchyard. Perhaps it was somebody who did not care; traditionally it was a wayfarer found dead by the roadside in the parish. Normally it caused long faces when a parish found itself saddled with the expense of burying a pauper vagrant, but, according to John Richardson, the vagrant who was first to be buried in the churchyard of St John's-in-the-Vale, was buried with something approaching civic honours.

Slowly the churchyard filled, and no doubt the people of St John's would have been content to inter the new dead among the bones of the old dead, but about 1880 a new consciousness in sanitary matters spread through the land and touched this remote mountain church when the Rural Council called a halt to burials in the old churchyard, and, on grounds of public health, issued an ultimatum to the parish either to close the churchyard or extend it.

So they extended it, the folk of the valley subscribing the cash necessary to buy the land and build the enclosing wall. And there John Richardson spent many hours, almost gleefully anticipating his own rest in the shadow of the church he had built.

When he was struck down with a paralytic stroke which left him almost helpless, an effort was made to secure a literary pension for him, the prime movers being Mr Stafford Howard, of Greystoke; the Bishop of Carlisle, and Mrs Lynn Linton, the eminent Victorian novelist.

When he died in 1886, the entire valley turned out to pay their last respects, and were joined by many others from further afield in the sombre procession winding its way up the fellside road to the little churchyard beside the church and school he had served so well.

His grave is opposite the east window of the church, just outside where the old churchyard wall used to stand. Today it is seldom visited because memories of John Richardson have faded, except in his native parish.

14

Pearl Rivers and Pearl Fishers

The shell fish . . . conceive and bring forth . . . shell berries.

Where the sea birds fill the air with their cries and the sky with translucent wings, where, if you are lucky, you might see or hear a representative of a dwindling race, the natterjack toad, the river Irt, Mite and Esk share a common estuary sheltered from the often gale-lashed Irish Sea by the dunes which form the Ravenglass gullery.

For rivers with such majestic beginnings — the Irt born in the solemn grandeur of Wastwater; the Mite among the heather and peat bogs on Eskdale Moor, and the Esk in the rugged beauty of Esk Hause — the estuary is flat and featureless. By road it can be missed altogether, from the train it does not earn a single glance.

The gullery is the principal point of interest if one is prepared to ask the County Council for a permit to visit, and to obey all the rules when one gets there. Black-headed gulls, once farmed for their eggs, are now the spoiled darlings of all comers and all seekers after ornithological truth, and the common and Arctic terns, once the elite of the gullery have to fend as best they can. Fortunately, they survive. Indeed, it is fortunate that the gullery has been protected as a nature reserve, for Heaven only knows what would have happened to it, its birds and their eggs at the hands of the highly mobile public who rush to the seashore at week-ends today.

Sea winds sweep the dunes clear, adding daily a new pattern of riffles in the sand among the marram grass, and each morning brings something new to be seen: fresh tracks of rabbit, the meandering trail of a fox which passed this way hunting; the minute prints of a vole and the unmistakeable zig-zag trail of an adder, all proving that the gullery is not exclusively the haunt of birds.

Birds, animals, the occasional group of people (armed, of course, with official permits) populate the Ravenglass, gullery whose dunes once provided shelter for Roman galleys, for Ravenglass was one of the harbours the Romans used to support the supply lines of Agricola's conquest of the North in the first century AD.

The scene has changed little from the time the Romans arrived on their advance up the coast and found a native Celtic population living happily, probably peaceably, among the plenty that was available from hunting the land and fishing the sea and the swarming rivers.

They probably found some of the natives fishing for pearls; probably bought pearls from them, because British pearls were popular among the Romans. It is certain that there was a trade in pearls between Britain and Rome before the Julian invasion of 48 BC. At any rate a breastplate which Julius Caesar dedicated to the goddess Venus Genitrix in thanks for his great victories was adorned with British pearls.

Certainly Julius Caesar held British pearls in high esteem, but Roman writers had differing opinions about them. Tacitus wrote of them and said they were of "a dark and livid hue". Pliny was not very enthusiastic about them and said they were "small and dim, not clear and bright".

Whether any of these pearls came from Cumberland rivers is open to question, but since stone axes of an earlier age found their way from Langdale where they were formed and the Solway coast where they were polished to parts of Europe; there is little reason to doubt that pearls could find a way along similar trade routes in an increasingly commercial world.

Bede in the seventh century had a high opinion of the pearls of his native country and said that in the fresh water mussels of the rivers "they often find enclosed in them pearls of all the best colours — that is both red and purple, jacynth and green, but principally white."[1]

Pearls were not only used for personal adornment. They were considered to have medicinal properties, and, ground to powder or even swallowed whole were said to be conducive to health and beauty. Intermittently, pearl fishing has been an occupation of riverside Cumbrians for many centuries.

Queen Elizabeth I, having been told, or having said — as traditionally she is said to have declared — that "Caldbeck and Caldbeck Fells are worth all England else", backed that opinion by confiscating the Goldscope copper (and gold and silver) mine in Newlands from her implacable foe Thomas Percy, 7th Earl of Northumberland. She also acquired rights over the pearl fisheries of the area.

In the Charter of the Company of the Mines Royal (1564) the Queen demanded her tenth of the "pretious metals, a royalty on other metals and the preferment in bying all pretious stones or pearl to be found in the working of the mines". Proving that she, or somebody in her court, realised that not a great deal of pearl was to be won "in the working of the mines", the Queen retained the pearl fishing in her gift and granted to her great Admiral, Sir John Hawkins the licence to fish for pearls in the river Irt.

This seems to have been the favourite pearl river at the time because in the late sixteenth century William Camden wrote that pearls were found there in quite large quantities. "In this brook," he wrote of the Irt near Drigg, "the shell fish eagerly sucking in the dew conceive and bring forth pearls or shell berries. These the inhabitants gather up at low water, and the merchants buy them of the poor people for a trifle, but sell them to the jewellers at a good price. Further muscle pearls are frequently found in other rivers hereabouts."

West Cumberland rivers are not unique in their role as producers of pearls. River pearls occur whenever the fresh water mussel occurs and Urio Margaritifera is found in a great number of rivers. Local conditions, however, dictate whether the mussels will or will not bear pearls; Urio produces pearls in some rivers and not in others. Today it seems to be more productive of good pearls in Scottish rivers than anywhere else.

In 1692-3 Thomas Patrickson, gentleman, probably a scion of the Patricksons of The How in Ennerdale, was granted a charter incorporating "the Company of Pearl Fishers in these two rivers" (the Irt and the Ehen). This company is reported to have "employed divers poor inhabitants to gather these pearls, and obtained such a quantity as he sold to London jewellers for £800".[2]

The charter of the Company of Pearl Fishers was granted for fourteen years, but long before the expiration of that period the "divers poor inhabitants" seem to have cleared Urio out of the two rivers, for the company died.

As late as 1860 a German called Moritz Ungar had the pearl fishing concession, and by that industry and application for which his race has always been famous, took a large quantity of pearls from the Irt, Mite and Esk.

Pearl fishing in the three West Cumberland rivers must have given Herr Ungar an appetite for more and he visited Scotland and bought up all the pearls he could find. West Cumberland tradition has it that the German took pearls valued at £12,000 from his three West Cumberland rivers, but the truth of the matter is that that sum was his total take from our rivers, from the Tay, the Spey and other Scottish rivers.

However, Herr Ungar was thorough, and at the end of his operations in West Cumberland he was considered to have dredged the three rivers so thoroughly that the mussel beds had been completely exhausted. This could be so because pearl fishing in these rivers has been only sporadic since, and the Irt, Mite and Esk do not figure at all in more recent outbreaks of pearl fishing.

In 1881 John Birkett, a Workington solicitor, fishing for salmon in the river Derwent at Ribton Hall, picked up a large freshwater mussel and found two pearls in it. Those are the only pearls which have been recorded as having been found in the Derwent.

Another West Cumberland river achieved a sort of prominence for its pearls in the first quarter of this century. The Ehen, which flows out of Ennerdale and past Egremont to the sea first came into prominence as a pearl river when its pearl fishery, and that of the Irt, was granted to the Company of Pearl Fishers in the seventeenth century.

Nobody seems to know when the later chapter of the

Ehen's pearl fishing history started, the doubt arising because the operations were carried out in conditions of secrecy, either because of the fear of prosecution for trespass from riparian owners, or a secretiveness which was natural in men who were on to a good thing and did not want too many others to come and share it.

It is known that as early as 1898 pearls were found in the Ehen near the bridge at Wath Brow, but they were reported to be small and of little value. Shortly after this a writer in the *West Cumberland Times* blew the gaff on the new, secret, and apparently flourishing pearl fishery which had sprung up on the Ehen. He reported:

A bottle containing a number of pearls in a jeweller's shop window attracted my attention the other day, and, consumed with curiosity, I strolled into the shop to inquire why they were displayed unmounted.

I found they were all pearls, not from the ocean, but from the river, and that a local stream, the Ehen. They had been extracted, not from the oyster, but from the horse mussel which I had forgotten the Ehen contains in great qualities.

There are fishers for the pearls as well as for the trout and salmon in the Ehen, and periodically the jeweller receives a store of the tiny stones which the mussel as well as the oyster secretes.

One of the small ones, nine grains, was priced at 12s, and the smallest, because of its pinkness, was worth only 6s.

Now and again a fisher comes across a good find, and the jeweller gave the instance of one which was bought for £12 and sold for £25, the new purchaser in turn parting with it for £51. That was a 15-grain pearl, and a beauty at that.

In 1913 five pearls were displayed in the window of Rushton's shop in High Street, Cleator Moor. They had been taken from the Ehen at Wath Brow.

It was a Londoner who started the great 'pearl rush' of the 1920s; or if he did not actually start it, gave some impetus to a movement which was already afoot in the district. This man turned up at the Anglers' Inn on the shore of Ennerdale for a holiday and began asking the locals about mussels. He asked, he said, because he had seen a great amount of shells lying about in the fields by the riverside, which suggests that some sort of clandestine pearl fishery was already under way.

Later the local people saw him down by Woodhouse, clad in waders, searching the stream bed with the aid of an "opera glass' picking up the best shells and throwing them on to the river bank.

One evening the Londoner told one of the regulars at the Anglers' that he paid for his holidays by selling the pearls he found. When this became public the pearl fishing craze spread throughout the district. The pearls were like manna from Heaven in a district which was suffering from heavy unemployment because of the run-down of the local iron ore mining industry.

Men who had been fishing pearls 'on the quiet' for years, found they had company. From Hazel Holme upwards to the lake, both banks of the Ehen were lined with fishers; men feeling the river bottom for mussels with bare feet; men searching the bottom for mussels with glass-bottomed boxes. There was a certain amount of rivalry as some sought to fish a particular reach of the river, but this pearl rush got by without bloodshed. Money was made, but no fortunes. It was all grist to the mill in an area filled with people so notoriously improvident that a week's unemployment after a period of comparative prosperity found many of them completely broke.

There were stories of big finds, and just as many stories of men who fished for weeks and found nothing. Brothers Danny and Jim Delany filled three tin canisters with pearls, some large and valuable, which they sold for an undisclosed sum. But they told a friend that they had sold a single pearl for five pounds to a Whitehaven jeweller.

Another successful fisher was Tom Park, of Main Street, Frizington, who took thousands of mussels from the bed of the Ehen. He found that nearer the lake both mussels and pearls were small, but as the river approached the sea both got bigger. "Inside the mussel shells," said Tom, "was of a most beautiful colour."

One of Tom Park's pearls was sold to a Manchester firm who paid him four pounds which was a low price for that real rarity among freshwater pearls, a snow-white gem as big as a pea.

Another finder was David Scott, a jeweller from Cockermouth, who took a nice pearl just below Ennerdale Lake.

There could still be pearl fishers operating in West Cumberland rivers, but if there are, they keep very quiet about it. The Fisheries Department of the Rivers Authority would take a great interest in anybody they discovered searching the beds for mussels, as they do in anybody they suspect of poaching the dwindling fish population of the rivers. It is not that taking freshwater mussels is an offence under the River Authority's by-laws, but that any mussels, and the pearls therein belong to the riparian owners.

In Ravenglass and Drigg it is impossible to find a river pearl let alone anybody who will admit fishing for them, but the local feeling seems to be that the Irt, Mite and Esk were fished out, their mussel beds exhausted many years ago.

People around Cleator Moor, Frizington and Egremont remember the pearl fishing boom which was at its height during the General Strike of 1926, but nobody knows of anybody doing any mussel fishing today, although it is unlikely that anybody would tell if they knew the fishers were still going out.

Since the freshwater mussel has tremendous powers of recuperation as a species, and since it has survived literally centuries of fishing, it is probably still there in the rivers; perhaps, from lack of fishing, growing bigger and better pearls than ever it did before.

But wet days and nights in the river affected the pearl fishers as they did the poachers, and perhaps the new prosperity which came to West Cumberland, making it more attractive to work for a regular wage than to spend weary days up to the waist in river water getting mussels and rheumatism, accounts for the decline of pearl fishing.

Occasionally there are stories of off-comers arriving, fishing for pearls, and departing, but no stories of big finds sufficient to lure the locals away from the pubs, the television, bingo or the hound trails.

15

Another World

Where poets met for tryst
They meet no more

"This," wrote Ann Radcliffe about Thirlmere, "is a long and unadorned lake, having little else but walls and rocky fells starting from its margin."

Ann Radcliffe was writing in 1794, but it is small wonder that her disparaging comment was resurrected and given fairly wide circulation in the last quarter of the nineteenth century when Manchester conducted the campaign which was ultimately to result in the lake being turned into a reservoir for the 'Cotton Capital' — or 'Cottonopolis' which was the name coined by the anti-Manchester faction who seemed at one stage even to baulk at writing the proper name of the place in their letters to *The Times*.

Miss Radcliffe published her observations on a tour of the Lakes at the end of a book she had written about a journey through Holland and Germany. Since she did her tour of the Lakes in a carriage from which she did not descend unless seeking refreshment, she cannot have taken a really good look at Thirlmere, and her opinion, therefore, counts for little.

Her opinion, however, was valuable to Manchester's Waterworks Committee as one of the few, very few disparaging comments ever made about Thirlmere: as a piece of counter-propaganda to an enormous weight of opinion which was pressuring Parliament and Manchester to leave Thirlmere alone.

Ann Radcliffe used the eastern route, the only one passable by carriages, but the early Lakes enthusiasts preferred the western side of the lake, of which a later writer said: "This almost unparalleled line of four miles is not accessible to carriages. Horses may travel, and persons on foot. From Armboth, the Great How on the Dalehead side is the principal feature, finely diversified with rock and wood; Naddle Fell clothed with feathery larches, and Wanthwaite Crags in the distance. Contrasting with the larches, the indigenous yew clings in dark masses to the crevices of the rocks, and the various colours, lighted up by an afternoon sun, are superb."

Manchester did not lack allies. A writer for a Leeds newspaper on a fact-finding mission during the early stages of the Manchester-Thirlmere controversy was also strictly carriage-borne, and described the roads in the vicinity of the lake as "uneasy".

Roads were important in the controversy because one of the carrots dangled by Manchester was the prospect of roads with easy gradients circling the lake in place of the admittedly undulating highway the Kendal-Keswick traffic had to negotiate in passing Thirlmere.

If the Leeds journalist was pro-Manchester it was providential that he and his party should meet a poor woman toiling up one of the steep ascents of the road past Thirlmere and crying: "For Heaven's sake, masters, will you give me a penny. I have walked from Kendal, but these dreadful roads have nearly been the death of me. Oh, I was never on such dreadful roads, and if you value your comfort you will not go any further."

The journalist did not say whether or not he gave the poor woman the penny she craved, but he ought to have done for her opinion backed his comment which was: "These are the roads about which there has been such a loud outcry . . . Manchester Corporation intend to circle the mere with good roads, as easy in gradient as the mountainous character of the district will allow, and as these roads will be at some height on the hillsides, an uninterrupted view of the water will be obtained. The finest prospects are from the western shore [he had been told], and this portion of the scheme will open out that side of the mere to vehicles and horsemen as well as to pedestrians, to whom it has been almost exclusively confined, and consequently some of the grandest views of the lake have

The 'Rock of Names' beside the A591 past Thirlmere. The scratched initials of Wordsworth and Coleridge have almost entirely weathered away

Dalehead Hall, a small Lakeland manor house which grew up around a seventeenth-century statesman's home

(*above*) Thirlmere; (*below*) Thirlmere Bridge, looking north
(nineteenth-century drawings by Thomas Allom)

been known to comparatively few people."

The 'new' roads around Thirlmere are certainly, as Manchester had promised, "easy in gradient"; their engineers certainly knew how to use a spirit level. But in a decade or two Manchester's afforestation policy around Thirlmere ensured that those "finest prospects" and "grandest views" were effectively screened from view and are only now beginning to emerge under Manchester's 'liberalisation' policy with regard to its Lake District property.

The A591 from Dunmail Raise, until it takes its dive down into Thirlspot, has about it an air of unreality in a Lakeland context; it does not seem to belong. It is not a scenic route; it is a place where you are trapped in your car or bus between walls with wire fences and trees; a treadmill of a road moving at the speed of the car or the juggernaut in front. Occasionally there are glimpses of the lake through the trees, but the road engineers stuck so rigidly to their contour that the many twists and bends make it imperative that the driver must concentrate on his driving. On this road this is not difficult; the scenery can hardly be said to be distracting, much less entrancing; it is one of the least attractive bits of road in the Lake District.

The 'scenic' route which opened up the western shore of Thirlmere does not succeed in exposing some of the "grandest views of the lake", as promised, although it is a road for more leisurely motoring, the myriad potholes inhibiting any tendency on the part of the motorist to hurry. Here the air of unreality is reinforced in the provision, nailed to the trunks of soaring conifers, of nest boxes for bluetits! It has often been suggested that Manchester's afforestation policy on the Thirlmere property resulted in a drastic fall in the local bird population. Having put up some nesting boxes, Manchester cannot be accused of not trying to right a wrong.

Righting wrongs seemed to be part of the policy of the Manchester Waterworks committee in post-Ullswater, pre-regional water board days; they changed their monoculture afforestation systems, planting more broad-leaved and less Sitka spruce trees; they encouraged public interest in their

Lakeland holdings; they even made a forest trail up Launchy Ghyll which was the cause of one of the more violent outbursts against 'Manchesterisation.'

Nobody better earned the right to speak for Lakeland than Canon H.D. Rawnsley, and anybody who interfered with its natural charm generally heard something to their disadvantage, whether they were day visitors who broke a fence or "mighty corporations whose undeveloped tastes riot in crude colour schemes of Reckitt's blue" (referring in this case to a rather unfortunate Manchester experiment with colour-wash on some of its Lakeland property.)

This was 1910 when the worthy Canon had given an edge to his temper in a brush through the columns of the *Manchester Guardian* and the local newspapers with local sporting landowners who, to make easier their sport of shooting rabbits had made "chess-board patterns of bracken-clad slopes", referring to the practice of scything-off square patches of bracken to make open spaces into which rabbits could be chased by the beaters.

When, that year, under Manchester's afforestation scheme around Thirlmere, the great oak trees of the woodland at Launchy Chyll, the last surviving piece of the original forest which had surrounded Thirlmere prior to the Manchester invasion, had been put to the axe, Canon Rawnsley believed it to be an "inexcusable spoilation of a fascinating feature of the Lake District".

"Where," he asked, "are the thrushes and the blackbirds to build now? Every branch had been a possible home but for the axe. I have many a time heard thrushes singing from these lower branches, and watched the squirrels playing upon them. I shall hear and see them no more."

Rawnsley knew that it would take a very long time to replace the beauty which had been effaced, and thinking about the oak wood which had been destroyed conjured up the mighty shade of Wordsworth who had also grieved over the loss of a wood at Ullswater where "the axe indiscriminately levelled a rich wood of birches and oaks that divided a favoured spot into a hundred pictures", and because he had heard the old people of Wythburn say that a squirrel might have gone from their chapel to Keswick without alighting on the ground.

Rawnsley and Wordsworth would like better what is to be seen at Launchy Ghyll today although they would both have fits of the horrors at the look of the lake itself when Manchester's thirst and a dry summer combine to half empty the lake leaving a deep ring of moonscape rock and gravel which seems as sterile as the steelworks slagbanks at Workington on the coast.

Thirlmere is 'different'. Manchester has seen to that. But it has always had an air of other worldliness about it, a special aura which gave it a status entirely its own in the hearts of the early Lakers.

It was a sort of never-never land which perhaps deserved the criticisms of the inhabitants of other dales who were themselves far from perfect. Thirlmere's legends, its traditions, its ghosts and its peculiar social history set it apart.

Although on, or easily accessible to the main highway running between Keswick and Kendal, the area around Thirlmere remained almost untouched by progress. People there lived their lives in their own way, the way that had been dictated by conditions and by centuries of forebears, just as people did in the more remote dales.

The lake, shaped like an hour glass with an ancient 'Celtic' bridge across the narrows for foot passengers – horses had to ford the shallows alongside the bridge – the almost feudal sway which the family of Leathes of Daleshead Hall held over their lands, and the mysteries of Armboth House where the Jacksons lived, gave the place something of its special character.

This was heightened by the status taken upon itself by the 'City' of Wythburn, a collection of steadings scattered on the opposite side of the valley from the church.

Close to the road which ran between Wythburn and Armboth, a few hundred yards south of Deer Garth Ghyll there was a large grey stone with a flat, sloping top. This was the 'Steading Stone' where, by tradition, the parish business was transacted and the manorial courts held. It was here that the "Pains and Penalties of the City of Wythburn" were enacted, the by-laws of an ancient parish parliament which listed the penalties to be paid by any-

body who turned out more sheep on the fells than he was
entitled to from the number of stints he possessed with his
farm. As an example, Bank Farm, property of the Hinde
family at the time of the Manchester take-over, had 39
acres of land, and 24 stints on Wythburn Fells, which, at
10 sheep to a stint, allowed the Hindes to pasture 240
sheep on the fells.

The Pains and Penalties also listed fines for allowing
horses and cattle to stray on the roads, and for defiling the
becks by throwing dead carcases into them. Manchester's
punishment for anybody found defiling the becks feeding
Thirlmere could possibly have been more stringent than the
original Pains and Penalties.

When Manchester bought Thirlmere and the land around
it, the Waterworks Committee found itself saddled with the
not-too-onerous duties associated with the lordship of the
manors of Wythburn and Legburthwaite, and as Lord of
the Manor, in trust for the Corporation, nominated Alderman John Grave, the then chairman of the Waterworks
Committee, who, as a native Cumbrian and a man with an
inclination towards social climbing, was probably highly
delighted. How seriously he took his position nobody seems
to know, but Manchester, for all its high degree of organis-
ation might have found it difficult to make provision in its
budget for certain of the obligations the Lord of the Manor
of Wythburn had to perform. For instance, he had to keep
a stallion, a bull and a boar for the common use of the
retainers and copyholders.

Stallion, bull and boar notwithstanding, Manchester was
kind to that part of its property which was not drowned
by the risen lake nor covered with conifers, for its farms
remain farms, complete with Herdwicks, and these farms
and the Corporation's other property remain firmly out of
reach of people wishing to buy farms as 'investment'
property or other moneyed off-comers seeking week-end
cottages in Lakeland.

On the lower slopes of Armboth Fell, now submerged by
the lake, was the Web Stone, so called because it was here
that webs of homespun cloth were sold or exchanged at the
time of the great plague of 1665, the inhabitants of the

valley feeling that moving their market out on to the open fellside was a just precaution to take against importing the plague into the valley. It is assumed that the webs of cloth, like the valley, were plague-free, and it must also be assumed that the dalesmen took precautions against importing plague on either goods or money. Traditionally, coins were sterilised by dipping them in a mixture of vinegar and water.

Strangely there are no legends or traditions about the Cop Stone, a large boulder, similar to the Bowder Stone which balances precariously on a small base near Launchy Ghyll.

Clark's Lowp was a huge rock a quarter of a mile from the head of Old Thirlmere, a name recalling a valley tragedy which the dalesmen characteristically contrived to turn, in years of telling and re-telling the story, into black comedy.

Clarke, after whom the Lowp was named, was saddled with a nagging wife who made his life so miserable that he climbed to the top of the crag which overhung the lake, jumped into the water below, and drowned. Less than broken-hearted, his wife coolly remarked that he had often threatened to do away with himself, but she thought the fool would never find the courage to do such a thing.

Sim's Cave was a place marked out on the fellside as the refuge of a man the dalesfolk believed had robbed and murdered a Dalehead man whose body was found in the lake. No proof could be found of the guilt of this "ill hang-gallows of a tailyer" who lived at Folnside, but the local people, convinced of his guilt, had their own methods of administering punishment, which, though falling short of straightforward lynching, were uncomfortable enough.

By implied threats and the broadest of broad hints whenever they met the man whether it was on the road or at the local inn, they made life for him so miserable that he eventually took refuge in the cave on the fell before the rigours of a hermit's life and the difficulty of getting supplies from a hostile population eventually forced him to leave the district for pastures new.

Other-worldliness was almost a way of life at Thirlmere;

the people of other valleys said the folk of Wythburn seldom knew — or cared — what day it was.

Walking from Grasmere to Keswick one fine Sunday morning in 1875, a man stopped to admire the view where the road approached the margin of the lake. Enchanted by the scene: the green valley of Wythburn, the mirror-still lake with the ancient Celtic bridge creeping over it with its three spans, and the tree-crowned hills and heather-clad rocks around, the visitor stopped to take it all in. And then the Sunday stillness was broken by the sharp click of a hammer striking stone some distance up the fell. Looking around, the visitor could see no sign of life, but eventually an aged dalesman came along the road. The walker asked the dalesman what could be making the noise which was now coming fairly frequently from up the fellside. The old man listened earnestly for a few seconds and then replied: "Oh, it's nobbut Turner wa'en a gap."

Those were the days when people in the Lake Country dales mostly remembered the Sabbath Day and kept it holy, so the visitor, shocked somewhat by somebody repairing a fellside wall and thus flagrantly breaking the Fourth Commandment, asked if people thereabouts usually did that sort of work on the Sabbath. "Nay, nit they," replied the man. "Abbut Turner's likely fergitten 'at it's Sunday." When the visitor said that he thought it strange that a man should forget the one rest day of the week, the old dalesman bridled: "Nut at aw! It's nut lang sen his next nebbur set off t' Keswick market wid a basket o' butter on a Sunday mwornin', an' niver food oot it was Sunday till he met fwoak ga'an to t' kirk."

Down where the edge of the lake used to be, well below the level of the present reservoir, lie the footings of the walls of Armboth House which formerly belonged to the Jackson family who also owned a small estate called the Grange, recorded under their name in the Crosthwaite registers from the very beginning of that record in the sixteenth century.

The superstitious local population probably had fewer regrets at the inundation of Armboth House than about any other part of the lost world around old Thirlmere because they held a firm belief that it was haunted. Tales were told of supernatural visitors, midnight lights; of a nocturnal marriage and a murdered bride, and of ghostly banquets and midnight orgies in which all the local ghosts were said to join, including, it must be said, the Skulls of Calgarth.

The Calgarth Skulls were said to inhabit a niche on the staircase at Calgarth Hall on the shores of Windermere as a grim reminder to, if not retribution on, the Philipsons who owned the Hall. One of the Philipsons, it is said, coveted the estate of an aged and eminently respectable couple. He trumped up a charge of theft against the couple, and as a consequence had them executed, which put them out of the way of his designs on their property.

Afterwards their skulls appeared at Calgarth and defied all attempts to get rid of them. They were thrown out, buried, burned, reduced to powder, but they always returned to their niche on the staircase until at last the Philipsons had them walled up in their niche, a solution which seemed to satisfy even the skulls because there were soon no Philipsons left at Calgarth for them to annoy.

The legend of the Calgarth skulls and the ghostly revels at Wythburn House inspired Alexander Craig Gibson to write one of the better poems based on Lake Country lore, better if only because Gibson wrote tongue in cheek and did not strive, as so many did, to give their folklore-in-verse the stamp of Sir Walter Scott's epics. Gibson wrote:

To Calgarth Hall in the midnight cold
Two headless skeletons crossed the fold,
Undid the bars, unlatched the door,
And over the step passed down the floor,
　　Where the jolly round porter lay sleeping.

With a patter their feet on the pavement fall,
And they traverse the stairs to that window'd wall,
Where out of the niche at the witch hour dark
Each lifts a skull, all grinning and stark,
　　And fits it on with a creaking.

Gibson takes his now-complete skeletons on their ghostly march:

Through Calgarth Wood, o'er Rydal braes,
And over the pass by Dunmail Raise . . .

Onward they go to "Wythburn's lowly pile" where other
ghosts join them, and so to Armboth Hall where the festivities
are in full swing behind windows glaring with light, until

On Rydal isles the herons awoke:
A pattering cloud by Wansfell broke;
The grey cock stretched his neck to crow
In Calgarth roost that ghosts might know
    It was time for maids to be waking.

And so the Calgarth skulls on their skeleton bodies flew
like the wind back to Calgarth, laid down their skulls and
rattled their way back whence they had come.

Dalehead Hall on the opposite side of the lake to
Armboth House was high enough to avoid the fate that
befell Armboth, and survives as a guest house for Manchester Corporation, and as a memory of a small Lakeland
manor house which grew up, over and around a sixteenth-
century statesman's home. The old can still be found
blending with the newer parts of the building, but the
whole is almost exactly as the Leathes family left it when
it was sold to Manchester. Only the old oak-studden door
has gone, a door so spectacular in the density of the oak
studs that covered its front that it merited mention by
several writers.

Thirlmere has had several names. It was Leatheswater,
the name taken from the family who owned so much of its
shore so long; Bracken Water or Brackmere, no doubt from
the prevalence of that mountain weed in its environs.
Hutchinson called it Layswater, a phonetical miscalculation
from 'Leatheswater'; Thomas Gray made a similar mistake
and called it Leeswater, and it has also been known as
Tirlmeer and Wyborn-water.

"The lake," wrote Gray, "looks black from its depth,
and from the gloom of the crags which cowls over it,
though really as clear as glass; it is narrow, about three
miles long, resembling a river in its course; little shining
torrents hurry down the rocks to join it, but not a bush to

overshadow them, or cover their march; all is rock and loose stones . . ."

Hutchinson, who seems to have decided that the old Celtic bridge across the narrows of the lake actually provided a dividing line between two lakes — one his Brackmere, the other his Layswater — wrote: "For romantic mountains and wild scenes, this stage [along the post road from Wythburn to Legburthwaite] affords the finest ride in the North of England, the whole road lying in a narrow and winding dell, confined by a stupendous range of mountains on either hand. In some places the vale is not wider than merely to admit the road, in other places it opens in little amphitheatres and again is shut in various forms."

And Hutchinson, like Grey, paid particular attention to the waterfalls waxing lyrical about them:

As we wander by the feet of these lofty hills, creeks filled with wood here and there afforded beautiful though narrow landscapes through which little rivolets, arising from the sides of mountains, poured down their hasty and noisy streams. The rain which had fallen the day before improved the beauties of the place . . . and at one place we could discern nine cascades falling from eminences which we conceived were near a thousand feet in perpendicular height. Where some of them came from the very brows of the hills, they appeared like strings of silver; advancing further spread into sheets of foam, and before they had made half their progress to the vale, tumbled headlong from precipice to precipice with a confused noise.

Most visitors to the original Thirlmere seem to have been impressed by the waterfalls tumbling down the fellsides, and even now they can, some of them, be glimpsed through the dense forestry which clothes the fellside giving a slight indication of the grandeur of long ago when Hutchinson saw nine waterfalls from a single viewpoint.

In "An Ode to the Sun" by "Mr. Cumberland", Hutchinson quotes:

Thee, savage Wythburn now I hail.

By any standards, Wythburn would not be considered

savage today, unless by a school party from Bolton committed to climbing Helvellyn from the car park by the church on a wet day.

The little church stands, demure, almost always empty, and always, apparently, freshly whitewashed; seemingly more a marker for the start of the Helvellyn walk than Wordsworth's "modest house of prayer", and lonelier today since its nearest neighbour, that low, unpretentious and apparently innominate building on the other side of the road was demolished, unmourned, unmissed, and without protest from anybody, early in 1972. But, in its own way, that building was famous for this was the *Nag's Head* — the primmer Victorians preferred to call it the *Horse's Head* — probably the best-known hostelry between Grasmere and Keswick.

The church could not interfere with Manchester's plans, although there was a suggestion at one time that church and churchyard might be inundated; but the *Nag's Head* and its effluent disposal problems did not accord with Manchester's idea of a pure water supply, and so it was closed down and turned into a store-room for the water-works.

In its new image, Manchester discreetly demolished the old inn, and so carefully built the road-verging wall that replaces it, that you can hardly tell where the *Nag's Head* used to be.

Manchester has its faults and, inevitably, its critics for what happened to Thirlmere, but few of the latter among the long-term residents of the watershed area because Manchester employs more people on its waterworks and forestry than were ever employed on the little farms of the area; is probably a much better master than any of the Leathes family ever were, and does provide dwellings for retired workmen and tenants, like the National Trust, making it unnecessary for their pensioners to leave the scenes of their lives and labours when their working days are over.

Critics, still unpacified by Manchester's more liberal policy over their Lake District property, and unimpressed by the tremendous lengths to which the Waterworks Committee went to obliterate from the landscape any marks made by their recent 'raids' on Ullswater and Windermere need to be told that it was a native Cumbrian who started it all: who gave Manchester the idea of drawing water from Thirlmere. This was John Grave, one of seven sons of a Cockermouth saddler who went to Manchester and made a fortune as a paper manufacturer. He also went into local government, was thrice Lord Mayor of the Cotton Capital, and was chairman of the Waterworks Committee in 1876 when the quest for water to quench the thirst of the city's people and industry began.

A clever, though unqualified engineer, Grave saw the possibilities of Thirlmere, and in a report to the Waterworks Committee, the consulting engineer, Mr J.F. Bateman said: "In addition to Ullswater and Haweswater, there is only one other lake whose elevation above the sea is sufficient to give a supply of water by gravity — this is Thirlmere, and it has been suggested (by your chairman, Mr Alderman Grave) that all the water which Manchester may require may be obtained from thence at less cost than from any other source."

Of all the lakes, obviously Ullswater was the one most favoured by the Waterworks Committee if only for its size, but, Grave pointed out, Thirlmere was 65 feet higher above sea level than Ullswater, although 163 feet lower than Haweswater, which was also being considered. But Thirlmere had 30 per cent more rain annually than the Haweswater watershed, and the fact which eventually won over the hard-headed Mancunians to Grave's Thirlmere scheme was that it would cost £170,000 less than the Ullswater scheme. Bateman's report stated that if Thirlmere was raised 50 feet it could supply 50 million gallons per day "for about 160 days continuous drought without rain". And that was after allowing 5½ millions gallons per day of compensation water to flow down St John's Beck.

Of course the announcement of Manchester's plans for Thirlmere was not greeted with universal acclaim. The Bishop of Carlisle, the novelist Octavia Hill and Canon Rawnsley were among those who lined up for the fight against this assault on Lakeland's natural beauty, and local property owners seemed determined to fight like tigers.

Thomas Leonard Stanger Leathes the 'squire' of Dale-head Hall imposed a ban on anybody with connections with the proposals entering his property, but Grave was nothing if not persistent, and a picture emerges, from the rather stilted terms in which the history of the scheme was later written by and for Manchester, which would have delighted the anti-Manchester faction if they had known about it at the time.

Finding it imperative that a survey be made of the lake shore, Grave himself embarked upon it in the company of Sir John James Harwood. If they were caught on Dalehead property the least they could expect was to be ordered off, and the worst a charge of buckshot in their backsides if T.L.S. Leathes was as militant as he had sounded.

Grave and Harwood, therefore, were discreet. They crept along more than half a mile of lake shore on hands and knees on a day which, even for Thirlmere, was "very wet". They accomplished their mission, but they both caught very bad colds.

If there was some sort of poetic justice in these two distinguished men being made bedfast for a few days, the Lake District was to inflict an even greater retribution on John Grave a few years later for his hand in the Thirlmere scheme.

As chairman of the Waterworks Committee, Grave was chief spokesman for Manchester in the wordy battle which raged over the scheme. When the Bishop of Carlisle cried out against "the substitution of engineering contrivance for Nature in her most primitive and untouched beauty", Grave replied: "nature has been at work for ages destroying her most primitive and untouched beauty. Perhaps the Bishop prefers the swamps and bogs which Nature always tends to make whenever she has a chance."

Once the Thirlmere scheme was under way, Grave returned to live in his native county. He built The Towers at Portinscale and proceeded to live the life of a country gentleman on a fortune estimated at fifty thousand pounds. He maintained his personal interest in the Thirlmere scheme and was a frequent visitor to the dam, and he was so obsessed with his brainchild that, it is said, he had a sample

load of every sort of stone which went into the Thirlmere
dam and waterworks built into The Towers.

But Grave was not yet finished. He had already created
an impression in the district with his great wealth, his
house, his servants, but perhaps success had gone to his
head for his next project was to become the greatest joke
Portinscale had ever enjoyed.

Although The Towers was well endowed with 'service'
buildings, Grave determined to build a new coach house
and stables. For a site he chose the low land between the
road and the lake below the village ignoring the advice of
the locals that the ground was too soft. On that ground he
built his coach house and stables "big as a church", in fact
borrowing a great deal of its design from church architec-
ture. It was a vast affair, with an enormous square,
four-storey tower, borrowed from the design of a fortified
Border church, and two steeples at the other end which
were said to be copies of the little steeple of Camerton
Church, near Workington. One side of the building, where
the coaches were kept, looked like the start of a set of
cloisters, and the walls were pierced by windows as well as
by ventilation slits which looked as if they had been
intended for defence by archers.

Load after load of the best stone and finest timber that
money could buy were delivered at the site, and still the
local wiseacres shook their heads and said, "That ground's
too soft." Local opinion generally backed up this judgment
and the building soon became known as Grave's Folly.

Folly it certainly was; the villagers were correct. The
ground was too soft, and soon after the walls of the Folly
had gone up, there were signs that the water of Derwentwater, seeping into the peaty ground underneath was
pulling it down again.

And it was pulled down, all except a small portion of
the gothic-arched coach-house which stood until a few
years ago in use as a cattle shed, providing something of a
puzzle for antiquarian-minded visitors who saw the frag-
ment and wondered why an obviously (from a distance)
monastic ruin should be missed from the maps and guide
books.

John Grave died in 1891, three years before the Thirlmere water scheme was inaugurated with great ceremony by Sir John Harwood who had shared with Grave in the adventure of trespassing into Dalehead property when they were still considering the feasibility of the scheme.

If the local inhabitants were cynical of the chances of the survival of Grave's coach-house, the people around Thirlmere were equally so about his water scheme considering that there was not enough money "in aw t' wurld" to take Thirlmere water to Manchester. But they were wrong. The first stone of the dam was laid in August, 1890, and the water was turned on in October, 1894.

Canon Rawnsley, who had been one of the leaders of the fight against Manchester, buried the hatchet long enough to be a guest of honour at the opening of the aqueduct and the banquet which followed. He said a poem he had composed specially for the occasion; and dedicated to Sir John Harwood:

> Our generations pass, our names decay,
> The spirit lives — the courage and the skill
> That chains the torrent, that can pierce the hill
> And lead sweet-water floods from far away;
> And tho' this vast laborious essay
> May fade in new adventure, men shall still
> Honour the heart and praise the stubborn will
> That brings strong purpose to its goal today.
>
> For you had gauged the future, felt the stress
> Of that great city's toil and thirst and strife,
> And when men's tongues were clamorous and loud
> You held commune with the silent cloud,
> You trusted Atlantic waves to bless,
> And claimed from Cumbrian hills their gift of life.

This seems over-fulsome comment, inbuing Harwood with qualities which fall somewhere between godlike and Wordsworthian, but the strangest thing about Rawnsley's participation in the jollifications over Thirlmere is not that he actually saw some good in the scheme, but that he was there at all.

Of course he had his regrets which he put into verse and which, he was careful to announce to the local newspaper editors, he would like to see published alongside his Tribute to Harwood. He called it "Thirlmere – Loss and Gain", and it went:

Farewell! the dear irrevocable shore!
Dark firs, and blue-bell copse, and shallowing bright!
Stern Raven Crag is cheated of its height,
Gone is the bridge the Romans crossed of yore;
The stately wain with Benjamin before,
The pack-horse string now fade from fancy's sight,
The "Rock of Names" has lost its guardian right –
Where poets met for tryst they meet no more!

Rawnsley seems to have been convinced that the old 'Celtic' bridge which crossed the narrows of the lake with its three spans was as old as its name suggested although neither he nor anybody else had any evidence that the Romans had ever set foot on it. It was of the 'classic' Celtic form. In place of arches there were three passages to allow the flow of water down the lake between stone-built piers which were connected by wooden bridges each with a handrail. Both ends of the bridge were connected to points above the high water mark on the lake shores by a wall of rubble masonry covered on top with flat stones to form the walkway. From end to end the wall and Celtic bridge extended 120 yards.

If Manchester displayed some callousness in destroying or submerging some of the focal points in the lore and legend of Thirlmere, it also showed some feeling for preservation.

On Black Crag beside the old turnpike road was the famous 'Rock of Names', famous even in the 1880's when work started on the Thirlmere dam. Here were carved the initials of William Wordsworth, his sister Dorothy, his wife Mary and her sister Sarah Hutchinson; his brother John (who died at sea in the wreck of the Earl of Abergavenny in 1805), and Samuel Taylor Coleridge. The occasion was a picnic held on the spot, and Rawnsley was convinced that it was John Wordsworth who insisted that they all leave their marks, and so earnestly did they apply themselves to what today would be labelled vandalism that the initials were still visible and readable when Black Crag was threatened with inundation.

Manchester decided to rescue the Rock of Names from a watery grave and present the rock to the Wordsworth Institute at the poet's birthplace, Cockermouth, as being the right and proper place for it. But the Rock of Names crumbled on being lifted and the relevant bits with the initials of the poets and their friends were built into a cairn which looks like a miniature of something between the Matterhorn and Napes Needle on the Helvellyn side of the road.

And there it stands today, most of the initials still readable to anybody prepared to go and look at it. But a visit to the Rock of Names is both arduous and dangerous. Yellow lines forbid parking near it; indeed forbid parking the whole length of this 'new' road. So that a visit to the Rock entails a walk of some difficulty through the Manchester Corporation forestry or of considerable danger along a road on which pedestrians are regarded by the majority of travellers (in motor cars) as trespassers.

When Manchester sited the Rock of Names where it stands today it preserved the rock and its celebrated graffiti as surely as if it had placed them in a strong room. Had the rock been easier to reach, the initials of Wordsworth and his friends and relatives would long ago have been obliterated by other, more modern versions of 'Kilroy was here.'

In passing it must be mentioned that if Manchester had carried out its original intention and handed the Rock of Names over to the Wordsworth Institute at Cockermouth it would almost surely have disappeared as the Wordsworth Institute has disappeared. Cockermouth is, or was, notoriously careless of its antiquities and it almost allowed the poet's birthplace to be pulled down to make way for a bus station!

At the top of the pass, Dunmail Raise marks the boundary between Cumberland and Westmorland, the name belonging to the heap of stones which, traditionally, marks the last resting place of Dunmail, 'Last King of Rocky Cumberland' who lost his last battle there. However, Dunmail is buried elsewhere because he is said to have died much later on a pilgrimage to Rome.

Visitors with treasure on their minds often ask if the

great heap of stones at the top of the pass has ever been excavated. The answer is that officially it has not, but that unofficially it has. When Manchester imported great gangs of Irish navvies to dig the three-mile tunnel under the pass for their aqueduct, some of them dug into the cairn in the hope of finding treasure. It is assumed that they found none on the unreliable basis that they would have told somebody in authority if they had. At any rate, being the courteous gentlemen these labouring Irishmen always were, except to each other in the local inns on Saturday nights, they rebuilt the cairn "much better than it was before".

The improvement of Dunmail's Raise aroused horror in Canon Rawnsley and others in the burgeoning society for the protection of the Lake District, and eventually the workmen were placed at great pains to reduce the newly-tidied cairn to something approaching its original scattered form.

So we may be certain that the cairn we see today bears little relationship in shape, or even in size, to the original. It is said that the repentant Irishmen added "a few more" stones which they collected from the fellside to make up for the damage they had done to the ancient cairn.

Notes and References

Ninian's Valley (pages 15-24)

[1] The Rev. Robert Walker, 'Wonderful' Walker, earned his soubriquet when he was priest at Seathwaite in the Duddon Valley for his industry and frugality which enabled him, out of a stipend which never exceeded seventeen pounds a year, to amass a fortune exceeding £2,000. He was priest, teacher, scrivener; he clipped sheep and spun and wove their wool; he helped the local farmers with harvest and sheep clipping. He raised a numerous brood of children, and lived until he was passed 90. It is said that his pattern for life was formulated when he was schoolmaster at Loweswater. Here, according to Wordsworth's *Memoir*, by the assistance of a 'Gentleman' in the neighbourhood, he acquired, during leisure hours, a knowledge of the classics, and became qualified for taking holy orders. Here too, an extremely low income forced him to keep a diary of his expenses, however trifling. Wordsworth says: "The large amount at the end of the year surprised him; and from that time the rule of his life was to be economical, not avaricious." The school at which Walker is said to have taught at Loweswater is the cottage at the foot of the Vicarage Brow.

The Singer of the Song (pages 39-48)

[1] Gilpin, Sidney. *Songs and Ballads of Cumberland.*

[2] Joseph Falder died in 1816, and his obituary in the *Cumberland Pacquet* of Tuesday, February 20 reads: "The 11th Inst at Cockermouth, in the 86th year of his age, Mr Joseph Falder, a man of no ordinary talents and ingenuity, who surmounted the disadvantages of a defective education, in no inconsiderable degree, by the native powers of a vigorous intellect. His manners were distinguished for unaffected modesty and artless simplicity; and his conversation was rich in anecdote, which he related with appropriate and characteristic humour. His temperance was so remarkable, that it almost rivalled the abstemiousness of a hermit; and though he deviated from the ordinary track of theological opinions, he was conspicuous for the purity and rectitude of his character, which even the voice of slander hesitated to assail with the slightest imputation. In fine, he was a philosopher in various acceptations of the word; in the regularity of

178

his conduct, the equanimity of his temper, the modesty of his demeanor, the integrity of his character, and the variety and compass of his knowledge; having made himself acquainted with the mathematics, and with natural and experimental philosophy: to which may be added a correct taste in the elegant arts of painting and engraving."

Valley of the Black Diamonds (pages 62-73)

[1] "George Smith was a native of Scotland; a man of genius and learning; but of an assuming air, irritable temper, and suspicious principles as to religion," says Hutchinson, quoting the *Biographia Cumbriensis*. "After being some time an assistant in some seminary of learning in London, he lived with and assisted Dr Desagulier in his philosophical experiments. Marrying soon after, he engaged in an academy at Wakefield, afterwards lived at Brampton; and finally settled near Wigton, where he lived on a small annuity but from what source it was dervied, was never known. He instructed several persons in that neighbourhood in Mathematics and Philosophy, and was a great contributor to the Gentleman's Magazine. Both he and his wife died at Wigton. He had the merit of exciting, in that neighbourhood, a very general attention to literature; and the demerit of promoting a spirit of suspicion and infidelity. He had a daughter, Mrs Sarah Smith, who, for some time, was a preacher among the Quakers."

[2] The need-fire was a custom which was a throw-back to ancient pagan rites. As its name suggests, it was used when it was needed: when 'the murrain' or foot-and-mouth disease struck a district. The fire was kindled in the 'old' way, by rubbing two sticks together, but first all the fires in the village had to be put out. Then a fire was made of wood gathered from the forest, a strict need-fire rule being that none of the fuel was to come from under the shelter of a roof. When the fire was burning, encouraged to make a great deal of smoke by using green, leafy boughs, the stock of cattle was driven through it. Farmers had even been known to drive their wives through the need-fire. If another district required the need fire, it was carried from village to village as a blazing torch, but always the recipient village had to ensure that all fires had been doused before its arrival.

Heamly Dance, Teun, Teal or Sang (pages 83-90)

[1] The 'bedgoon' had nothing to do with bed. It was a type of dress, probably modelled on a night-dress, which had been adopted by the countrywomen.

[2] The maskers were strolling players, mostly local youths and men who performed a play dealing with the triumph of good over evil, and called in some places *Alexander and the King of Egypt*. It survived into modern times as the 'Mummers' play' which went the rounds of the village houses at Christmas.

[3] The *Cherry Tree* was sacrificed when Manchester built the Thirl-

mere dam and inundated it. The *Nag's Head* survived as a store for the waterworks until 1972 when, unmourned, and almost unnoticed, it was demolished.

[4] Gibson, Dr A.C. *Folk Speech of Cumberland and the Counties Adjacent*. Gibson was a native of Whitehaven, practised at Ullock and at Coniston, and led a nineteenth-century revival of interest in the dialect.

[5] Pronunciation of the dialect is difficult for the non-Cumbrian who finds the double vowel particularly hard to master. In this line of Gibson's poem are three of these double vowels which are sounded as if the letter 'y' has been inserted, as hyamley, tyun, and tyal for heamly, teun and teal. The 'a' is always hard, the 'u' always broad. Take 'teal' as an example, and separate the 'e' from the 'a', pronouncing it as 'tee' and 'al' (as in allow). Say 'tee-al' as two syllables and quicken until they become one, and the 'y' sound inserts itself, and we have the dialect word for 'tale.' 'Heamly' is homely, and 'teun' is tune.

Will the Real Betty Yewdale . . .? (pages 99-111)
[1] A significant inclusion in "The Doctor" is the original story of "The Three Bears", Southey's intruder into the bears' domain being a nasty old woman. Goldilocks was a later invention.

The Man Who Loved Herdwicks (pages 122-132)
[1] Nicholas Size kept the Victoria (now the Bridge) Hotel and the Buttermere Hotel and wrote a fictional account of a struggle between the descendants of the Norse settlers of Buttermere and the forces of the Norman William II. *The Secret Valley* is still widely read. Size also wrote *Shelagh of Eskdale*, another quasi-historical novel. He is remembered locally for his campaign against the local Rural District Council who opposed his wish that he should be buried at his beloved Buttermere. He won, and his remains lie in a grave on Nixon How above the church.

Ghosts, Rank Upon Rank (pages 133-134)
[1] *C. & W. A. & A. S. Transactions*, New Series, No. xiii.

The Vale of St John and Poet John (pages 140-151)
[1] Hutchinson's *History of Cumberland* says:

Long after the conquest, this parish [Caldbeck] was forest and waste, and parcel of Allerdale. And an highway or main road from Westmorland and the Eastern Parts of Cumberland to the Western coasts of this country, having run through these forests and wastes, they lay long under the imputation of being the resort of such free-booters and dangerous outlaws, as we suppose Robin Hood and his fellows to have been.

It was on this account that Ranulph Engain, the chief forester of Inglewood, granted a licence to the prior of Carlisle to build an hospital there for the express purpose of relieving such unfortunate travellers as were prevented from proceeding on their journey, either by the inclemency of the weather, or by having fallen into the hands of the desperate banditti aforesaid.

On this grant the prior inclosed some portion of the forest, in the environs of the hospital, which stood near the place where the church now stands: but, though it was thus inclosed, the right of the soil still remained in the Lord of Allerdale, whose authority was necessary to keep lawless multitudes, by whom these woods and hills were haunted, in some degree of subjection and order.

[2] His "newspaper just twice a week" was the old *West Cumberland Times* which came out on Wednesdays and Saturdays, and in which a great deal of his dialect writing was first published.

[3] Susannah Blamire (1747-1794) born at Raughtonhead, a pioneer of Cumberland dialect writing, author of numerous poems, and co-author of others with Katherine Gilpin. Sidney Gilpin, who edited *The Songs and Ballads of Cumberland*, wrote that she "possessed the most original and reflective mind that Cumberland has produced — always excepting the revered name of William Wordsworth."

Pearl Rivers and Pearl Fishers (pages 152-158)
[1] *Hist. Ecc.* i, ch. 1.

[2] Nicholson and Burn, *The History and Antiquities of the Counties of Westmorland and Cumberland, 1777.*

Index